The Contrarian's Guide to Church Planting

By Carl Kuhl

Edited by Daniel S. Ferguson

1

This book is dedicated to Deena Kuhl.
Mom, you inspired me to read and write. Thank you.

Table of Contents

Introduction

STARTING FROM SCRATCH

Most of what you know about church planting is wrong. Dead wrong. No, seriously. You may think you have some idea what it's like to start a church. You get some money, you get some people, you get a location, have at least one singer/guitarist and one preacher, and *voila*, a church is born. That's so far from the truth, it's painful.

The reality is that planting churches is *hard*. And not just difficult, though that's certainly part of it. I mean that it will feel like running into a brick wall—repeatedly. The number of barriers that will simply jump in front of a new church is staggering. Some of them you might be able to think of, like money and resources, but many are ones that nobody, not even pastors, can see coming.

But that's not what this book is for. This is not a how-to book. This is not a theology book. This is not even a spiritual growth book. I offer no details on building a launch team or raising a million dollars. Nor will I argue the missiology of church planting based on the ecclesiological context of Paul. I won't attempt to inspire you to fall on your face in prayer or go on a forty-day fast. There are plenty of books on those topics; this simply isn't one of them.

So now that at least one of you is still reading (Hi, Mom!), let me talk about what this book actually is. Simply put, this is a reflection, not just on my own experience over the last decade of church planting, but on the many misconceptions that are out there about what it is like to start something from scratch and keep it multiplying.

There are two core convictions that inspire this writing, the first of which is...

Conviction #1: "The local church is the hope of the world."

I couldn't agree more. Jesus told Peter that he would build his church, and the gates of Hades will not overcome it (Matthew 16:18). I love that Jesus mentions Hades (the realm of the dead) in the same breath that he talks about the church. The church, after all, stands counter to death. We are in the resurrection business. Everyone spends eternity somewhere, and that somewhere is either Heaven or Hell. Jesus is the only hope that anyone has of escaping the natural, eternal consequences of their sinful choices. Since sin leads to death (Romans 6:23) and Jesus rose from the dead, Christ's is the only power that can resurrect people back to life. Not just eternally, but presently. Jesus isn't just the path to eternal life, but to the best life right now. That's the hope of the world.

And Jesus started the church and empowered it with his own Spirit to be the community of people sold out to Jesus and committed to his mission of saving people from both the present and eternal consequences of their sin. The church, we're told by Paul, is the very body of Christ (1 Corinthians 12:27). If Jesus is the only hope for the world, then that hope passes through us because he has chosen, for reasons beyond comprehension, to use these often ugly, truly messed up humans to carry forth his mission through the empowering of his Spirit. Without the church, there is no community wherein people can experience Christ's life-changing truth and grace.

Therefore, we need every church to be on mission with God: "to seek and to save the lost" as Jesus did (Luke 19:10). I love anything that makes churches better, stronger, and more effective at evangelism. Some churches have been doing that for decades, even centuries. But church plants hold a special place in my heart simply because they are statistically more effective at saving people from Hell. (There are some church planting books I recommend at the end of this, but one of the best is not technically a church planting book, but is still amazing: *Hell Is Real (But I Hate to Admit It)* by Brian Jones.)

Consider these numbers from Ed Stetzer:

- Churches under 3 years old win an average of 10 people per year for every 100 members.
- Churches 3-15 years old win an average of 5 people per year for every 100 members.
- Churches over 15 years old win an average of 3

people per year for every 100 members. (*Planting New Churches in a Postmodern Age*, p. 6)

Just based on those numbers alone, it appears that new churches are more effective at reaching the lost. Thinking about this for just a moment proves its truth: If I'm starting a new church, I have to reach new people with the Gospel, or I won't have a new church! But as I win new converts, I must divide my time between discipling them and still pursuing unreached people. So by its very nature, a new church is more effective at reaching the lost.

> # Bottom line: If we want to reach the lost, we have to plant more churches.

Conviction #2: Most of what you know about church planting is wrong.

Okay, so maybe *most* is a little extreme. Perhaps a more accurate statement would be that much of what you know about church planting is wrong. To explain this better, let me tell you my story and our church's story.

How I Went From Punk to Pastor

Everything was going fine until I became friends with a bombmaker, got busted for driving illegally, and nearly got expelled from school for fighting—all in one semester.

I grew up in a Christian home with solid parents. They had the wisdom to get us into a great church where we could all grow in Christ, and I gave my life to Jesus at a young age. I've found out that when people hear I grew up in church and in a Christian home, they ask if I ever had a time of rebellion. My answer is, "Well, I *tried* to rebel; I just wasn't any good at it."

My rebellion wasn't the typical partying and drinking. Instead, I just had fun breaking rules. This came to a head my freshman year of high school, when the following events occurred:

- In October, I got kicked out of my high school for buying a bomb on school property. (It was only technically a "bomb." In reality, it was a firecracker. But boy did the school enjoy calling it a bomb.)
- In November, I got the genius idea to regularly steal my dad's car at night and drive it around town without a permit, much less a license.
- In December, I got into a fight at school. Well, that's what the administrators called it. It was a one-sided pounding. I had the savant-like wisdom to call a 6'6", 230-pound freshman with not an ounce of fat on his body something bad. He punched me one time, I flopped over like a cheap tent, and it was over.

Needless, to say, I had a lot to think over during my Christmas break that year, since all I had the chance to see for two weeks were the inside of my bedroom's four walls.

As I laid there, looking at my ceiling, I thought, "Carl, you're not very smart. You're trying to just have a good time, but you're not very good at it."

So I decided that instead of going to church just to hang out with my friends, I would try to actually do what I was being taught there. I guess you could say this was my second conversion. I accepted Jesus as my Savior when I was seven, but I didn't acknowledge him as my Lord until I was fifteen.

I had the privilege of growing up in a fantastic church, so when I was ready to grow, my church helped me do just that. Our youth group was amazing, and our lead pastor was the best preacher I've ever heard. I couldn't go to church and not be challenged to follow Christ more closely. Our church's top priority was evangelism, and that manifested itself in a few ways. Obviously, we heard the Gospel in sermons, but that wasn't all. We also saw the Gospel in attendance growth as the church became one of the largest in the country (and even still continues to grow today). But the way it grabbed me most was in challenging me to be personally evangelistic. Largely through my high school pastor, Jim Burgen, I came to see my public high school as my mission field. And we saw several of my classmates baptized over the next few years.

But the evangelism for me needed to go to another level, so I decided to attend Bible college and go into ministry. After college, I wanted to get an experience a little different from what I'd grown up in, so I went to a smaller, much less traditional church, where I worked for four years. It was self-supportive when I arrived, but in many ways still felt like a church plant: we met in a high school, had some leadership transition right before I arrived, and we figured things out as we went. That church helped open my eyes to the world of church planting. In fact, my boss told me explicitly, "Carl, whenever you leave, I'm going to be really mad at you...unless you leave to plant a new church!"

The church I grew up at then hired me as their Resident Church Planter (I promise that's a real title), and we ended up doing a parachute plant in Maryland. That means we didn't have a launch team before we moved, didn't know who would come to our church, and didn't even have a clue where we'd meet. We just selected the general area, moved there, and launched a church. Of course, it's a little more complicated than that, and I'll share some more details later in this book, but my point for now is that we didn't have some great story of a launch team of a thousand people where I'd been living for years with lots of local contacts and a church building waiting for us to use.

We gradually recruited a launch team of just over thirty people, and on September 14, 2008, Mosaic Christian Church was born. I experienced the thrill and depression of most church planters as our opening day attendance of 143 quickly sank to averaging less than a hundred.

But we grew from there. In 2011, we moved into a renovated warehouse as our first permanent facility and have continued growing to where we average 1200 people each weekend. We have sent dozens of mission teams overseas, we sent one full-time missionary to Bolivia, and helped start five other new churches in our region. We are a vibrant community that connects in groups and gives time and money to kingdom causes, passionately pursuing those who need the hope and grace of Christ in their lives. Most important, we have baptized 600 people in the last 10 years. And as I write this, our $10 million, 1000 seat building is under construction that we'll move into this year, as we anticipate even more of the above in years to come.

All that to say this: our church plant has made it. We aren't on life support as many church plants I know. We haven't closed our doors; and we are, in fact, thriving as God continues to bless us. That was, and continues to be, our story, not that the perfect person led the perfect church, but that Jesus took a chance on an impenitent punk, transplanted him and his family to an unknown area, and grew a church from nothing, impacting thousands for the Kingdom.

What Comes Next

The following pages reflect my perspective on church planting based both on my experience and what I have read and seen in others. Before we launched, I read every book on church planting I could find. I attended the best church planting conferences. I lived, breathed, and slept church planting. And I think 90 percent of what is out there on the topic is spot on. In fact, I hope you are doing all those things, too: listening to experts, visiting conferences, and reading books. Yet I still believe that we are limiting God's kingdom by putting some unnecessary conditions and expectations on church planters.

I'm not expecting you to agree with everything I say. But this book will offer you the wisdom that will force you to grapple with questions you probably haven't thought about, while at the same time encouraging you that maybe God does in fact want to use you in great ways.

Again, these are my opinions, but they have been tested at Mosaic, and I have seen them true in other contexts as well. If you will allow me, I think you will be very encouraged that God wants to use you in a great way. And in order to see that, you must understand that **the most popular statement about church planting is dead wrong.**

Chapter 1

THE MOST COMMON ADVICE IN CHURCH PLANTING IS WRONG

I was playing Ultimate Frisbee when I first met Cincinnatus. Going to college was a great experience, and one way we had fun was to go to a park next to the Ohio River and play. In that park, among the trees, concrete steps, footpaths, and riverbank, I encountered a huge statue of Cincinnatus handing the *fasces* (a symbol of ruling power) away with one hand, clutching to a plow with his other.

Here's the backstory. Cincinnatus was a humble man. *Humbled* would be the more accurate term, actually, because after his son was convicted of a crime and executed, Cincinnatus had nothing left but his farm. As he recovered from his grief, he grew accustomed to the daily lifestyle of tilling his soil and growing his crops. He finally managed to get his life under control when three neighboring tribes attacked his town. And who did they turn to for help but the farmer Cincinnatus? They asked him to lead the Roman armies against the tribes, and he received the *fasces*, the symbol of ultimate power in Rome. After leading his people to victory and securing their continued freedom, however, Cincinnatus handed back his absolute authority and returned to work on his farm. America today still celebrates this stunning act of humility with statues and various organizations that bear his name, one such group, the Society of the Cincinnati, residing near Mosaic in Washington, D.C., in the famous Dupont Circle.

Cincinnatus did not set out to become a political leader or savior of his people. But when the time came for him to lead, he did so with valor, strength, and wisdom. He showed his humility by rescinding his power after the battle was over. It brings to mind that famous line from Shakespeare: "Be not afraid of greatness; some are born great, some achieve greatness, and others have greatness thrust upon them" (*Twelfth Night*, Act II, Scene v).

Years ago, when a city began on the banks of the Ohio River, its founders asked, "How do we want this town to be known?" They remembered the story of Cincinnatus and said, "We want to be a town of people who are wise enough to rise to the occasion when needed, yet humble enough not to pursue power for power's sake." They named it the town of many Cincinnatus-es. We call it Cincinnati.

I believe that God has puts thousands of Cincinnatus-es in place across this country and millions around the globe for the purpose of rising to the occasion of planting a church. However, there is one huge problem: **They are**

told they can't do it.

The Fallacy of the Calling

The first thing everyone tells you about church planting is that you must be called. They say this over and over again in books, at conferences, at boot camps, and everywhere you turn. And the people who say this seem to have Scripture on their side. They tell of God's visit to Abram, Moses at the burning bush, Joshua seeing the angel of the Lord, and Jeremiah's vision of God. Then in contemporary Christian culture, we hold up this idea of a very spiritual call and have people share their stories of dramatic, life-changing moments when God called them.

The problem with that is we use it to limit people who can effectively lead for God's kingdom by telling them they have to have had very dramatic encounters with the divine to be qualified. You can almost sense in some cases that people try to one-up another person's call by making theirs more exciting or sensational. And many are told they can't plant or lead a church because they aren't "called."

> # We have over-spiritualized "the call" to church planting.

I think we need to stop using Moses, Abram, and Gideon in this way and instead look at a person who had no direct calling but still made a huge impact for God's people. You know him as Jonathan.

The story begins with evil winning the day. Saul is the king of Israelites, the Israelites are God's chosen people, but the pagan Philistines are in control. In fact, there are only two swords in the whole nation: King Saul's and that of his son, Jonathan. God had chosen Israel to be a light to the nations, but evil was ruling over the people. This isn't much different than the world we live in today. God has chosen the church to be a beacon of light in this world, but when we look around it seems that evil is ruling— abortions, divorce, physical abuse, boys refusing to become men, drug abuse, financial ruin, and greed seem to reign supreme.

When Jonathan looks at his situation in Israel, he thought, "My Dad is king, but things aren't right here." When I think of the issues in our world today, I think, "Christ is king, but evil has an awful lot of control here on earth." Jonathan needed, and we need, to do something about it.

My favorite part of this story is that **Jonathan answers a need, not a call.** He didn't see a burning bush like Moses. Jesus didn't appear to him and call his name like he did with Paul. Jonathan simply said, "Evil is reigning, and that's not right. Somebody's gotta do something. Might as well be me."

When I was in high school, I had a specific call to ministry. But I've never felt a specific call to church planting. But then in college, I read *What's So Amazing About Grace?* by Philip Yancey. He tells the story of a social worker in Chicago who had a woman come to him seeking help. She was distraught. She had no home. She had no food. She had, instead, a drug addiction, one that had become so expensive that she became a prostitute, selling her body to afford drugs. The woman came to the social worker crying while she confessed this, explaining that the drugs had become so hard to afford that she had resorted to renting out her two-year-old daughter. She could make more money in a couple hours that way than she could by working herself all night. After blurting all this out, she looks at the social worker and asks, "Can you help me?"

This guy doesn't know what to say, so he finally asks, "Did you ever think of going to a church for help?"

The woman catches herself and says, "Church? Why would I go there? I already feel bad enough. They'd just make me feel worse."

I had two reactions to that story. First, she's wrong! She's either seen a televangelist who sounded greedy or been to a judgmental church that doesn't practice Christ's teaching or simply doesn't know. Either way, she's wrong. She's never been in some of the great churches I've been to.

But then I realized the dread truth: This woman has never been to a good church. And neither have most people. Did you know that in 1900, there were 28 churches for every 10,000 Americans, but as of 2004, there were only 11 churches for that number? And despite megachurches, the average church size hasn't changed much in that time. That means there are fewer churches for more people, and it means that people like that drug addict aren't aware of a grace-filled, relevant church where they can find hope.

God sometimes calls people in a burning bush experience. But we need more Christians who will simply say, "This isn't right! I'm not waiting for someone to be called. I'm just going to do it!"

Jonathan said it like this:

> *Jonathan said to his young armor-bearer, "Come, let's go over to the outpost of those uncircumcised men. Perhaps the Lord will act on our behalf. Nothing can hinder the Lord from saving, whether by many or by few"* (1 Samuel 14:6).

Jonathan does something absolutely extraordinary, and in comparison to how we treat church planting today, what Jonathan does is so contrarian. Jonathan assumes that God has called him to fight. See, our default today is to wait for God to call us. But God has already called us! He's told us to make disciples, to seek and to save the lost. God has already told us that he's more excited about one sinner coming home than a huge Christian concert with 50,000 voices singing to him.

We look at all those great stories of Moses, Gideon, and Paul and think that's how God works. But I maintain that **just because God has worked through direct callings doesn't mean God will always work that way.** The Bible, after all, is a collection of exceptions, not norms. Part of the reason the great calling stories are in the Bible is *because* they're amazing and out of the ordinary. But one of the reasons we have the Bible is to know that God has called us to be on mission with him. We've all *already* been called. Signing up for salvation means signing up for the mission of the Kingdom. No exceptions.

In his famous essay, "Politics and the English Language," George Orwell suggests that we rid our lexicon of every word and idiom that has outlived its usefulness. Similarly, I believe that we need to retire the excuse that "God hasn't called me" for not planting churches.

Just think about other stories in the Bible. David didn't wait for a call to fight Goliath. He just wondered why no one else was doing it, so he stepped out himself. Nehemiah didn't wait for a call from God to rebuild Jerusalem's walls. In fact, *he* called on *God* to rebuild! So instead of waiting for a divine, bush-burning experience, our default mindset needs to be waiting for God to stop us instead of standing still and waiting for God to start us. Don't ask if God is calling you. Look instead for ways that he may be stopping you.

Three Qualifiers to Consider

Now before you immediately put down this book and say you're all in to plant a church, let me point out three qualifiers that Jonathan puts on himself and that you should consider before jumping in head-first.

Qualifier #1: What does Kramer Think?

Remember the episode of *Seinfeld* where Elaine dances? I know I'm dating myself a bit, but since the reruns are on about 17 times per day, I'll assume the answer is Yes. George describes it as "more of a full-bodied dry heave set to music." She's such a horrible dancer that no one wants to tell her. Finally, the always honest Kramer blurts out, "That ain't dancing, Sally...you stink!" Elaine confronts Jerry, and it's only when he can't escape that he admits, "You're beyond stink!" Elaine responds, "But I really enjoy dancing!" Jerry quips, "And that's not helping either."

No matter who you are, you have someone who believes you should start a church. Maybe it's your mom, your spouse, or a disgruntled member of your current church. But never base your opinion on whether you should start a church on these people.

Find Kramer.

The way Jonathan did this was to ask the guy carrying his armor, "What do you think?" This was a great person to ask. An armor-bearer's job was to carry Jonathan's battle supplies—maybe a shield, probably his sword—until it was time to go into battle. When asked, he would have to hand these supplies to Jonathan so he could fight. The armor-bearer would be stuck there with no weapon, hoping his boss would fight well so they would both live. So the armor-bearer has no other motive for his answer than his life. If he's wrong, he dies, plain and simple. And what does the armor-bearer tell Jonathan?

"Go ahead; I am with you heart and soul" (1 Samuel 14:7).

Remember first that we've decided that we're called until God says No, and that we're not waiting on him to initiate. But as you're considering if God is calling you *not* to plant a church, the first thing to do is to ask the Kramers in your life. Who are the people who will be brutally honest with you? Your boss? The church you grew up in? A college professor?

This is why I believe in the assessment process. In preparing my plant, my wife and I attended an intense, three-day assessment that involved a psychologist, counselors, ministers, little sleep, group projects, and a complete inventory of our life history, including talking about pornography, sex, debt, and education. And yes, *we* paid *them* for this experience. You couldn't pay me to go back to that assessment today, but it was one more Kramer that spoke into our lives and encouraged us when we still weren't sure were cut out for this church planting thing.

This is the first qualifier, but let me give a qualifier to it. Don't just go to one Kramer and do whatever s/he tells you. The Bible says there is wisdom in many counselors (Proverbs 15:22), so go to many Kramers. In fact, one of my friends was told at the assessment that he was too young to plant, but he had so many other Kramers telling him to go ahead that he did. Ten years later, that church averages over 1200 people per week, has baptized hundreds and has sent more to be the core group of another church plant. That happened because he had enough Kramers in his life to make him believe that God wasn't telling him No.

Who is a Kramer? They're simple to understand but difficult to find. Basically, a Kramer is someone who tells you the truth and is behind your mission, but isn't impressed by you. They see what you're doing for the Kingdom of God, but they're enamored with Jesus and not you.

Qualifier #2: What's the Plan?

In the United States, we love a great underdog story. We enjoy seeing Rudy, the Titans, or Seabiscuit overcome great odds to win in the end. Even spiritually, we love seeing people overcome seemingly insurmountable odds through the power of God.

> # There is a difference between being an underdog and being stupid.

Every church plant is an underdog story. Every church plant faces huge odds against success. So don't add to that by not having a plan. In fact, if you don't have a solid plan that others believe in, I believe that's God telling you No. Look at Jonathan's plan:

> *"Come on, then; we will cross over toward them and let them see us. If they say to us, 'Wait there until we come to you,' we will stay where we are and not go up to them. But if they say, 'Come up to us,' we will climb up, because that will be our sign that the Lord has given them into our hands"* (1 Samuel 14:8-10).

Basically, Jonathan set up a plan. "If they say this, we'll attack, but they say this, God doesn't want us to." He doesn't waste a month drawing up something too detailed, but he doesn't fly willy-nilly into a shower of arrows that would get him killed either. He had a strategy. He knows if they attack from the higher ground he won't be able to defeat them. But if in their arrogance, they invite him up to level ground, then he will win.

So come up with a plan for your church plant and show it to the Kramers in your life to see what they think. At the minimum, your plan should show the following:

- How much will this church plant cost? Show how every dollar will be spent.
- How much money needs to be raised in advance?
- Where will this money come from?
- What consultants, coaches, and companies will you employ along the way?
- How big of a launch team do you need?
- Where will you get this launch team?
- What's the plan if you don't get that amount of people? That amount of money?
- What staff will you hire, at what point, and who will pay them?
- What is the vision of your church?
- What core values and practices will drive this new community?

There are tons of questions you could ask on top of that, too many to list, but the point is that the plan needs to be more than just a 30-second, off-the-cuff presentation on why you should plant a church. Jonathan had a plan to attack the Philistines. David had plans drawn for the temple. Jesus had a plan of how the world would be evangelized. You should have a solid plan, too. Numerous tools exist to help you make this plan. Boot camps, conferences, books, project managers, and coaches can all help you come up with a plan to test this qualifier.

Church plants already have the odds stacked against them. I have heard that three in five fail. So you are an underdog whether you want to be or not. But be an underdog; **don't be stupid.** So where's the plan? You need to come up with a workable strategy that doesn't require a miracle of God every single step of the way. If the plan is in place, then God is probably not telling you No on this qualifier. Yet there is one important question that remains about the plan.

Qualifier #3: Is it working?

I was in my head-to-toe pajamas eating Domino's pizza on the floor of my parents' bedroom when my life changed forever. I met E.T. I hung on every line he said, and still get chills when I see his last words: "I'll be riiiigghht heeerrree." Boom. Cinematic genius.

Spoiler alert: at the end of the movie, Elliot takes E.T. to the mountaintop to set up a communications device with his fellow aliens back home. When he gets it all set up, Elliot exclaims, "It's working! It's working!" And indeed it does, because E.T.'s family comes and gets him in a spaceship that paints rainbows.

Just like Elliot, as you begin the process of church planting you need to ask, "Is this working?" Preferably ask that before you go all in. You have to take baby steps to figure out if God is telling you No.

When I was a little kid, my mom made me join the swim team. I hated every second of it, and I'm still not sure I've forgiven her yet. But there was one horrible experience about it that wasn't her fault at all. It was mine. It was a typical practice, and we were swimming millions of laps. It became my turn to dive in, and I somehow got confused about what end of the pool I was in. I dove as if it were deep water, when in fact I was in the shallow end. The next I knew, SMACK! My head cracked on the bottom of the pool. I was a little dizzy and bloody, but at least I found a way to get out of practice!

I think too many church planters are like me at swim practice. They dive in all or nothing, and sometimes they crack on the bottom and come up not knowing what happened. That's why you have to take baby steps before you are 100 percent committed: to see if your plan is working. Jim Collins in *Great by Choice* says that great companies fire bullets, then cannonballs. He means that good organizations don't put all their eggs in one basket before they know if something will work or not. Instead, they take small steps towards the goal, and if those work, they take larger steps.

Before you argue that this means you don't have faith or aren't trusting God, go back to the story of Jonathan.

Jonathan climbed up, using his hands and feet, with his armor-bearer right behind him. The Philistines fell before Jonathan, and his armor-bearer followed and killed behind him. In that first attack, Jonathan and his armor-bearer killed some twenty men in an area of about half an acre (1 Samuel 14:13-14).

That plan was a bullet. Their response was another

bullet. The attack was a third bullet. Then they launch the cannonball:

> *Then panic struck the whole army—those in the camp and field, and those in the outposts and raiding parties—and the ground shook. It was a panic sent by God. Saul's lookouts at Gibeah in Benjamin saw the army melting away in all directions...Then Saul and all his men assembled and went to the battle. They found the Philistines in total confusion, striking each other with their swords. Those Hebrews who had previously been with the Philistines and had gone up with them to their camp went over to the Israelites who were with Saul and Jonathan...So on that day the Lord saved Israel* (1 Samuel 14:15-16, 20-21, 23a).

Similarly, you have to find ways to shoot bullets before you fire cannonballs to see if your plan is working. Here are some ideas:

- Raise just a little money.
- Recruit some launch team members or staff.
- Evangelize some non-Christians to see if they buy into the vision.

If you can't get early victories, it's likely that God is telling you No to church planting. Now it could be that he's just telling you No for this time or No for the role you're pursuing. Even if it's working, that doesn't mean it will be easy. It doesn't mean there won't also be some small losses along the way. But continue to ask if what you're doing is working. If it is, you'll likely be able to launch a church effectively.

The Better Question

Asking whether God has called you to plant a church is the wrong question. The better question is if God has called you *not* to plant a church.

Before our church moved into our first permanent facility, we needed to raise a minimum of $150,000 above regular giving. We called our capital campaign "What if...?" During the campaign, we asked questions like these:

- *What if* the church is the hope of the world?
- *What if* we show our faith?
- *What if* we can make the difference?
- *What if* we really worship?

These questions drove us to ask ourselves what really matters. Is it putting a new deck on our house or helping more people find Jesus? Is it going to Florida for vacation or baptizing a friend?

During this campaign, I learned about a branch of study called "counterfactual history," which tries to extrapolate what would have happened in history if you change certain events.

- What if Lee won the Battle of Gettysburg?
- What if Hitler had been killed in the assassination attempt of 1944?
- What if Al Gore won the 2000 election?

- What if Chipotle had never been invented? (Okay, that one's just mine.)

The actual definition says counterfactual history is "a form of historiography which attempts to answer 'what if' questions known as counterfactuals." Counterfactual history asks if something didn't happen, what would have been the result? We ask the same kind of question in a positive sense. What if a marriage can be healed? What if a soul can be saved?

This is a good exercise for us, to pretend that we're in the future looking back and asking, **"What if we do nothing?"** What if you only plant a church if you have a burning bush experience? What if you focus on yourself? What if you turn a blind eye to the lost? What if a divorce goes through? What if we don't start any more churches? What if we don't call men to their true role? What if we don't throw a Christmas party for kids who aren't getting anything else? What if someone goes to Hell?

The Pivotal Moment

Have you ever had a moment you knew was pivotal in your life? I know one of mine was in the mid-1990s. It has nothing to do with me. Our church did a capital campaign to reach more people, and during it, the mother of one of my friends was asked to get up on a Sunday morning and share her story of what she was giving to the campaign. She explained that she's a single mom with three teenagers. She worked at the church, so she wasn't exactly loaded. Her ex-husband didn't pay child support. So she held a family meeting and said, "Kids, I don't think we have any extra money beyond our tithe to give to this campaign."

The family sat there silently, and then my friend, Andrew, spoke up and said, "Mom, we have cable. We can give up cable." His mom was shocked. She didn't watch television much, only the kids did, but each said they would give up cable. As she concluded, she said, "That's not much money, but it is a lot of sacrifice, and it's what we can do."

Some of you, maybe most of you, reading this book need to give what you can to God's kingdom. He's not asking you to stay comfortable. He's not asked you to wait for a burning bush. He has commanded you to seek and to save the lost.

I believe that decades from now, people will look back at this moment in your life as a pivotal moment in eternity. People will say stuff like this:

- I just wanted to make money and get to the top, but someone who thought they were too old started a church, and I came to know Christ there.
- We had given up on our marriage. We had already divided up our stuff. But a college student didn't hear God say No. She helped get a new church started, and Jesus transformed our marriage.
- I was lost. I was going to Hell. But someone who didn't think they were cut out for it started a church, and Jesus saved me from my sins.

After learning about counterfactual history, I realized I didn't actually like it. It focuses on what could have been. I wanted to focus on what will be. I'm asking you to embrace the possibility that God has already told you his mission, and he hasn't told you No. What if you can make a difference just like Jonathan? Christians throughout history have made a difference. The Bible says we will make a difference, and with the power of God's Spirit, you will make a difference that lasts forever.

Now, if you think God hasn't told you No, I'll tell you why the most important gift in church planting is one you never hear about.

Chapter 2

DON'T BE A KNUCKLEHEAD

Raymond Zach apparently had a death wish. On May 30, 2011, he walked into the San Francisco Bay fully clothed. Someone noticed this odd behavior and called 911. Dozens of rescue workers showed up at the scene, but all they could do was watch. For an hour. All because the Alameda Fire Department's water rescue program was discontinued two years earlier due to budget cuts.

"[The] Alameda Fire Department does not currently have, and is not certified in, land-based water rescues. The city of Alameda primarily relies on the United States Coast Guard for these types of events," a police spokesperson said. The Coast Guard did dispatch a boat, but the water was too shallow for it. However, none of the other agencies on scene—not the Alameda County fire department, not the Oakland fire department, not the Alameda County sheriff, not the Oakland police, nor the East Bay Regional Park police district—went into the water to help rescue Raymond Zach.

"The incident...was deeply regrettable," Chief Mike D'Orazi said. "But I can also see it from our firefighters' perspective. They're standing there wanting to do something, but they are handcuffed by policy at that point." They were more concerned about following the rules than about saving somebody's life.

One man told the board during a meeting about the event that "It just strikes me as unbelievably callous that nobody there with any sort of training couldn't strip off their gear, go in the water, and help this person." Ironically, Zach's body was recovered by an off-duty nurse who swam out fifty yards to rescue him.

That story makes me embarrassed to be an American, embarrassed to even be human. But here's where I think the application lies for us as church planters: we are in the life-saving business. And to do that, we sometimes have to ignore the rules. I don't mean ignoring the Bible, and I don't mean we do whatever we want or that the end justifies the means. Instead, I mean that...

> # We should be more concerned about creating environments that save people than about how we've been told to do things.

Loving God with All Your Mind

Have you ever met someone who over-spiritualizes everything? Philip Yancey once wrote that he has friends who see an angel behind every open parking spot and a demon behind every red light. He's not sure whether he should envy them or pity them.

As church planters, we face the same temptation. We believe that the venture we are undertaking is very spiritual, carrying eternal ramifications, and that is true. But for some reason, we seem to dismiss a vital part of the tools God has given us to accomplish this mission.

Jesus says that the greatest commandment is to "Love the Lord your God with all your heart and with all your soul and with all your mind and with all your strength" (Mark 12:30). As church planters, we have to love with our heart as we emotionally worship. We love God with our souls as we ache for the lost to see God's kingdom come. And we love with our strength as we pull all-nighters writing sermons or get sweaty setting up our equipment. But I propose that **we're not very good at loving God with all our mind.** To explain what I mean, allow me to employ an old short story.

Do you remember the Sherlock Holmes story called "Silver Blaze"? It involves murder and a missing racehorse. When Holmes shows up, the inspector has already arrested someone, confident of his guilt. Of course, Holmes takes the clues and feels quite right about the alleged murderer. Then get his missing piece of information, which is recounted this way:

Gregory: "Is there any other point to which you would wish to draw my attention?

Holmes: "To the curious incident of the dog in the night-time."

Gregory: "The dog did nothing in the night-time."

Holmes: "That was the curious incident."

Holmes deduced that the dog must have known whoever was walking nearby, and that is the only reason it did not bark. That narrowed the suspects down to the guilty party. Bam, case closed, light up the pipe. Elementary, my dear Watson. It was that one missing piece of information—that didn't make any noise—that brought the solution.

That's exactly what our problem is today in church planting.

Let me explain. Over the past few decades, the spiritual gift that receives the most attention in church ministry circles is, far and away, Leadership. There are leadership books, conferences, webcasts, blogs, tweets, and lunches. Heck, there may even be a leadership line of clothing for all I know, like Rick Warren's Hawaiian shirts or custom glasses from Chris Hodges.

Either way, all of this emphasis on leadership is a good thing. No, I haven't worn any Hawaiian shirts. But I have read the books and attended the conferences, and they have definitely made me a more effective leader. And the gift of Leadership is essential to church planting. Leaders cast vision, raise funds, organize teams, motivate the disheartened, and help people take steps towards Christ.

Obviously, you can't plant a church without doing those things. Other church planting books will tell you, accurately, that if you don't have a leadership gift you probably should not plant a church.

However, there are a lot of problems in churches today because of a spiritual gift that doesn't make a lot of noise but is absolutely vital to success.

I'm talking about the gift of wisdom.

The Salsa of Church Planting

I love a good Mexican meal. Burritos, tacos, fajitas, chips, guacamole, sopapillas. I'll eat it all! But here's my theory: you can judge any Mexican restaurant as soon as they bring out the salsa. If the salsa's good, it's going to be a great meal. If it's not, get the check immediately. Why? Because the salsa, at least for me, goes on everything. If I'm eating a fajita, it's gotta have good salsa on top. Same with tacos, and of course chips. You can have great Mexican dishes, but without good salsa, I won't be back.

> # Wisdom is the salsa for everything we do in leadership.

You can cast vision, you can motivate, you can organize. But if you don't do all that wisely, you will burn people out and alienate the very people you're trying to lead. You'll sit in frustration, knowing you're a good leader and end up blaming the people you led for not following, when the reality is that it's your fault because you lacked the necessary wisdom to do it right.

Truth be told, you can have leadership without wisdom, but these will be the results:

- You'll raise a lot of funds...but you'll spend them very quickly.
- You'll organize a team...but they'll get burned out.
- You can build a great church...but they'll follow you and not Jesus.

Leadership without wisdom is fleeting, like smoke in the wind. The Bible speaks to the need for wisdom. It captivates three whole books in the Old Testament and hundreds of other verses, too. Here's a section about it from Proverbs.

Get wisdom, get understanding; do not forget my words or turn away from them.
Do not forsake wisdom, and she will protect you; love her, and she will watch over you.
The beginning of wisdom is this: Get wisdom. Though it cost all you have, get understanding.
Cherish her, and she will exalt you; embrace her, and she will honor you.
She will give you a garland to grace your head and present you with a glorious crown...
I instruct you in the way of wisdom and lead you along straight paths.

When you walk, your steps will not be hampered; when you run, you will not stumble. (Proverbs 4:5-9, 11-12, NIV)

I believe wisdom is the missing salsa in many church plants today. Yet, according to Scripture, wisdom is one of the easiest things to attain. James says if you lack it, ask God for it, and He will pour it out on you (James 1:5). But too often, in the fast-paced world of church planting, we have so much going on that we simply don't stop and ask.

Daily—yes, *daily*—before you start your endless to-do list, ask for wisdom. Because like vision, wisdom leaks. You can have it one day and then use it all up. Ask God for a fresh supply every day.

First, let me say what wisdom isn't. It's not some supernatural insight that comes from on high in blazing clarity. It's not a magic wand that you can simply wave at things and know the answer. But it is that weird inclination that makes you treat each situation differently. It's that gut feeling that you need to make a bold ask at this lunch appointment. It's that quiet confidence that you've done all you can do and that God will deliver you. It's that check in your soul that keeps you humble when you ask for the seemingly impossible.

Wisdom is the salsa of church planting. Always ask for more.

How Not to Over-spiritualize Everything
There are four primary ways that church planters commonly over-spiritualize things. Here they are, and

here's how to avoid them.

Way #1: For the love of money

When you ask many church planters how they will fund their new church, the response is often, "We are going to trust God." They say, "If it is the Lord's will, it's the Lord's bill." That's interesting.

Do you remember that YouTube video from auto-tune the news story about the bed intruder? One of his sweet lines is, "We got your t-shirt, and you done left fingerprints, and all of you are so dumb. You are really dumb!" When people tell me their entire funding plan is to "trust God," I want to put on a bandana and sing, "That is so dumb!"

I know that sounds mean and judgmental, but this book isn't a warm-and-fuzzy. It's a *contrarian's* guide to church planting. Besides, Jesus is on my side! Jesus says that if you are going to build something, you sit down and figure out what it will cost, because if you start construction and don't have the money to finish, everyone will laugh at you (Luke 14:28-30). Unfortunately, too many church plants have been funded with little or no money, and it ends up making the church fail, the senior pastor doubts himself, the launch team feels guilty, the lost stay lost, and the pastor's family becomes disgruntled.

I heard of a church planter in Virginia that was sent from a large, growing church with a grand total of $50,000 to launch a new church. The problem was that was all he had, and they wanted him to start a full-scale, quality Sunday morning worship service. The church set him up to fail. And of course, he did. That church is now closed, and the planter makes a living by working at a cell phone kiosk in the mall.

The problem is that we have all heard these amazing stories of a church that didn't know how it was going to make it week to week, and somehow God provided in an amazing way, and now it's a self-supporting, growing, huge church. That makes for a great story at a conference. It makes for a horrible pattern after which to model your church. Remember: **just because God has acted that way doesn't mean he will continue to act that way.**

Instead of blind faith, we need to ask, "What is the *wise* thing to do?" When it comes to finances, we need to test the waters of fundraising and set different parameters.

- We'll decide to plant only when we have x dollars committed.
- We'll move to the location of the plant only when we have y dollars in the bank.
- I'll only work part-time for the church until our weekly income is z.

Don't over-spiritualize money. In ministry, money is more like gas in the car than a perpetual motion machine. It's not magic; the more you have, the further it goes, and without it, you will be Fred Flintstoning it as far as your legs can push. It takes money to do ministry, plain and simple. If you don't have the money, you can't do the ministry. Be wise with finances.

Way #2: Location, location, location

It was the most encouraging story yet.

My wife and I were just beginning to figure out where we were going to plant. I had been hired by a church in Louisville as their "resident church planter". When we came to the agreement that I'd be there a year and then go plant they asked, "Do you have a specific place you feel led to plant?" I said "no" and they responded, "We'd prefer you to plant somewhere in the northeast: Washington D.C. or north."

That was a pretty big area with lots of major metropolitan cities, so it was a bit overwhelming. To help get some direction, I was calling other church planters to ask how they decided to plant where they were. The planter in Maine was the most inspiring.

He and his wife had done something similar a few years before, so they took an exploratory trip to Maine to see if they should plant there. When their plane landed, they rented a car and stopped at a gas station for directions. While the husband was picking up some ho-hos, the wife went to the cashier and before she could say anything the cashier blurted out, "I just wish God would put a good church here because I want one, and if there was one that taught the Bible, I'd go there in a heartbeat." The wife immediately explained why they were there, and by the time the husband got to the counter with his soda and ho-ho's, his wife and the cashier were in tears, praying together and hugging. The wife turned to her husband and said, "This is where we're moving!"

When I heard that I thought, "Sweet! We'll visit some cities. At the right moment, the clouds will part, sunbeams will shine down, and God will audibly announce in a voice sounding like James Earl Jones, "This is where thou shalt plant."

Okay, I wasn't expecting that, but I was still expecting a great "God story". I remember the first place we visited was a suburb on the north side of Baltimore and, remembering the guy from Maine, I approached another customer at Chipotle to ask: Do you know of any good churches around here?

You know what happened? The guy's eyes got wide and he said, "No, but I'm not really a church person and I've been looking for one—do you know where I could go?"

Not really.

In reality, he looked at me like I had broken out of the insane asylum and was going to infect him with a terminal disease if he talked to me for another three seconds, and without making eye contact he said, "Uhhhh, noooo," as he turned and walked away.

Ouch.

My wife and I ended up visiting numerous neighborhoods in five of the largest cities in America, and James Earl Jones (I mean, God) never did part the clouds and speak to us.

So we asked, "What's the wise thing to do?" For us, it was actually phrased like this: "Where do we *want* to move?" If we worked for GE and they were relocating us, where would we go? If the church failed and we were stuck living somewhere, where would we want 'somewhere' to be? When we want to take a break from church stuff, what city would we want to be in to have a good time? (Actually, we first asked: what area *needs* a new church the most? But we quickly threw out that question, because every area we looked at needed another healthy church!)

When we narrowed the search down to two places we took a look at demographics and showed them to some church plant experts, and they recommended one over the other, simply because they said it would have more people in our life stage whom we would better reach. And that's the really under-spiritual story of how we ended up planting in suburban Baltimore.

I will add one caveat to this. I am always skeptical when someone wants to plant in the same city as the church where they're already working. I'm not talking about when the church itself initiates the plant, because there are a bunch of success stories like that. However, I'm skeptical when a staff member tells the church, "I'm leaving to start a new church, whether you support it or not. And yes, God just happened to 'call' me to a place where I have dozens of people who are disgruntled with how you're doing things so they're following me down the street where I can do it better." I know that's not what they say...but that's what they're saying, right? I'm not saying God never calls someone to plant a church in the same city, but it just sounds too easy.

One pastor calls these people "church pirates". They swoop into a church, work there or get involved, and then feel "called" to start a church next door. The new church isn't really a church plant; it's a church transplant! It reminds me of Absalom stealing the kingdom from David more than it reminds me of Paul planting a new church in Lystra. I like when Paul said in Romans 15:20, "It has always been my ambition to preach the Gospel where Christ was not known, so that I would not be building on someone else's foundation."

If God has gifted you to plant a church, then plant a church; don't transplant a church. And use wisdom to figure out where to plant. (If you are considering planting in the same town as a church where you already work, I encourage you to pick up and read a copy of *A Tale of 3 Kings* by Gene Edwards.)

Way #3: Leadership

Have you heard about *The Three Ingredient Cookbook*? It's exactly what it says it is. Every recipe has only 3 ingredients. One of my friends got it as a wedding present when she was inexperienced in the kitchen, the idea being that even she would be capable of these recipes. But here's the thing about the 3-ingredient cookbook: if you leave out one of the ingredients, it doesn't work! Some recipes call for a dozen or more ingredients, and if you are out of a particular spice you can omit it no problem. But when there are only 3 ingredients, you need all of them!

This is how it is when it comes to leadership. I wholeheartedly believe in Bill Hybels' "3 Cs" of hiring: their competency at the job, their chemistry with the team, and the character of the person.

> # We romanticize character but underestimate the importance of chemistry.

Now let me be straight: I'm not suggesting we hire someone who is a chain smoker, addicted to porn, hasn't picked up his Bible in a month, and roots for the Pittsburgh Steelers. What I mean, though, is that we get so focused on character that we put blinders on to everything else. We will send a possible staff hire to assessment, we dissect the spiritual gifts of leaders, we look at giving habits to check their generosity, we do all kinds of things investigating character. But an important question is this: Do you want to hang out with them?

- If it's a small group leader, would you want to go to their house to hang out every single week?
- If it's an elder, is it someone you'd go on vacation with?
- If it's a staff member, do you want to be around them all day and eat lunch with them?

The best hiring advice I ever received was from Kyle Idleman. He said, "Carl, hire people who, when you pull into the parking lot and see their car, you think, 'I'm so glad I get to work with him/her today!'"

Why would I put a leader in place to be in a four-hour meeting with them debating finances, buildings, and vision if I wouldn't even want to go to lunch with them?

The stakes of leadership are too high to do this thing with people we don't click with. I'm not talking about excluding people who are capable and qualified. I'm just saying that if I'm going to be in the trenches with someone, it better be someone I get along with!

And don't think this is just about staffing. Wisdom says you've got to have chemistry with volunteers as well. In fact, you need to be willing to fire volunteers for the sake of the team. I know conventional practice is that you take free labor however you can get it. But if anyone—staff, volunteer, visitor, Christian or non-Christian—is destroying the unity or preventing others from accomplishing the vision, they've gotta go. Isn't this what Jesus says to the rich young ruler? He wanted to be one of Jesus' crew, to follow him around. But Jesus could only accept people who were sold out to the cause. So he said, "First sell everything and then come follow me." But he wouldn't do it, so Jesus wouldn't take him.

This also means you find ways to develop greater chemistry with your team. Go on vacation together. Have "Staff Fun Days". Go out to lunch...and don't let yourselves talk about church one time. Laugh together. Create inside jokes.

Then, when the busy or difficult times hit, it's not just business transactions that need to be made. It's getting in the trenches with those you love and working together to take ground for God's kingdom.

I Have a Confession

I'm not a closet alcoholic or a porn addict. But if you are a church planter reading this, then what I'm about to say probably breaks the "rules". It doesn't feel very leader-like. It doesn't feel like I am an adventurer, boldly going where no church planter has gone before. Here's my confession: I steal sermons. Probably three to five times a year, I will get someone else's sermon manuscript, swap out their stories for stories of my own, and preach it. And don't worry, I tell my church straight up what is going on.

A few times I've stolen entire series from other people. This does not sound or feel very spiritual, but in my case, it is most effective. There are times when I face the following choices: Do I want to give people something original or something that will most help them? And since for our first several years I preached over forty-two weeks per year, it seems like the logical thing to do. I can't come up with forty-five sermons that are better than what my favorite preachers can come up with! So what sermon series did I steal to open Mosaic's history with? It was an idea from a book I read several years ago from Andy Stanley, a book I highly recommend. The title is *The Best Question Ever*. When I picked it up I thought that was a pretty bold claim. When I put the book down I knew it was true. Based on Ephesians 4, Andy says that the best question ever is, "What is the wise thing to do?" We launched our church asking that question because we know that question will answer just about any question in life, and ultimately, it will lead people to Jesus Christ.

Besides, Andy Stanley didn't invent this question— God did! That's why so much of the Bible is wisdom literature. That's why there is a spiritual gift of wisdom. And that's why, I believe, we are commanded to love God with our minds.

So don't be a knucklehead; instead, use common sense. Because wisdom, when paired with leadership, can be an unstoppable force for God's power that will save those who are drowning in their sin before our very eyes.

Unfortunately, it's not just wisdom you need to plant a church. There's something else...and church planters lie about it all the time.

Chapter 3

MONEY, MONEY, MONEY

My palms were sweaty and my heart racing. I was trying to waste time surfing the internet, but nothing I did distracted me from the huge decision being made in the next room.

I had come on staff at the church as the resident church planter. The time had come for me to make my pitch to that church of how much I was asking them to contribute to our future church. They were our cornerstone partner. There was no network, no denomination. There were other churches, individuals, and organizations we were going to ask for money, but few of them had the giving potential of this megachurch, and none of them had the same relationship with me as this church did.

I had carefully planned how much our plant would cost, including salaries, equipment, location, rent, etc. (more on that later) and I had made a pitch for them to become our keystone partner. I knew the number I was asking for was more than they'd ever given to a church plant in their history. I was purposefully asking for more than what I expected to get.

So if they gave what I'd asked, or even close, our future church would be on the way to being funded well. But if they came in well below what I asked, I'd have to go back to the drawing board of how we were going to be funded.

I made my pitch. The team asked a couple basic questions. Then they asked me to step out of the room into my office, and they'd call me when a decision was made. So I sat nervously at my computer, praying to God that this thing would get funded.

Fundraising is maybe the first big challenge for every church planter. I once had a professor ask, "How much ministry can you do with 100 dollars?" We all answered with deeply poetic answers, but he answered: "How much ministry can you do with 100 dollars? I'll tell you how much: 100 dollars' worth!" It wasn't quite as deep of an answer as I was hoping for, but I see the wisdom in it now.

Ministry costs money. And church planting takes a lot of money. I've already stated that I believe that fundraising shows whether or not God has called you to church planting, so let me point out at the start the two methods of church planting this won't apply to: bi-vocational pastors and house churches.

Some people are very passionate about house churches. I am not very knowledgeable on house church funding, but the principles of funding still apply regardless of model.

What I'm saying should also be applied with a grain of

salt to bi-vocational churches. Personally, I'm not a fan of bi-vocational pastoring. It's hard on the church because it doesn't get the pastor's full attention. And it's hard on the pastor's family because it's difficult to not give yourself fully to ministry. Many bi-vocational pastors end up neglecting their wives in the name of serving God, and the wife gets embittered towards the church and either holds it inside and becomes numb or expresses it and causes dissension. In this scenario, both the church and the pastor lose.

So I'm addressing here those of you who are attempting to raise a lot of money to launch large.

***

To best learn how to raise money, learn from Frank Abagnale. (And no, I'm not talking about forging checks!) You may remember Abagnale from the Spielberg film *Catch Me if You Can.* He was a con artist who faked being an airline pilot, a university professor, doctor and attorney...all before the age of 22. He got his start by learning how to forge checks, thereby financing an extravagant, risky lifestyle. In order to travel, he then conned people into thinking he was an airline pilot who was trying to get somewhere else while he was off duty. He also faked being a doctor who oversaw a group of interns, but resigned from that after an incident with a child could have been fatal.

But the most intriguing thing to me about Abagnale was his stint as a (fake) lawyer when the Louisiana Attorney General employed him. Conning his way into being a ride-along pilot or committing check fraud seems possible, but how can you fake being a lawyer? Well, technically, he didn't fake it—he genuinely passed the Louisiana Bar Exam! Granted, he had faked his transcript from Harvard and he didn't know squat about practicing law. But the bar exam is the final test of whether one can practice law in a given jurisdiction. And Abagnale passed!

When asked how he pulled this off he responded, "It wasn't very difficult. Louisiana at that time allowed you to take the Bar over and over as many times as you needed. It was really a matter of eliminating what you got wrong and having the IQ I had and the memory I had, I could eliminate those things and go back and pass."

The problem with Abagnale, of course, is that in the end he was arrested and served time in France, Sweden, and the United States, before later agreeing to assist the FBI in fraud cases and opening his own security company. Here's the lesson from Abagnale:

> # If you try to be someone else, eventually it will catch up with you.

Now how does this relate to money and fundraising? Because the biggest problem I see in church plant fundraising today has nothing to do with the economy or size of gifts. Here's the biggest problem when it comes to raising money: People aren't themselves.

When our church sent our first mission team to Haiti a few of the team members were having trouble raising funds. The trip was going to cost about $2000, and our missions director had trained them to raise the money. But a handful just weren't having any luck.

I was asked to have lunch with them to see if I could help inspire them to raise more money. I sat down at lunch with these folks and asked what they had done so far. They each responded, "I've sent letters to everyone I know— family, coworkers, friends....and I'm just not getting much response!" I asked what else they had done, and when I heard "nothing" I was stunned. My shock wasn't from their lack of doing anything else. It was rather that these were possibly the two most social, most likable, most excitable people in our entire church. And they had just used letters? I told them immediately, "You two have the best personalities of just about anyone I know. If I'm giving to you, it's not because of some dry letter; it's going to be because I was around you, and you got me excited about this." So that's what they did: they arranged a couple of lunches, some dessert gatherings, some face-to-face meetings, and sure enough, they raised the money they needed.

So the contrarian advice to church planting is to be yourself. Too many denominations, sending churches, or church planting organizations have a plan for how you should raise funds for your new church that they want to impose on you. Definitely learn from these and use them when you can. I assume the reason they have these plans is that they've worked in the past. But don't raise money a certain way just because it worked that way for someone else.

My gifts are preaching and wisdom. So as we began

the journey of fundraising I wondered, "How can I use my gifts to get the best results?" We decided to create small environments that were personable where I could preach to people. We arranged a series of meetings that were catered with drinks and desserts. We let people know in advance we were going to share about our ministry opportunity and let them make a decision whether to join us or not. We didn't want a bait and switch where they showed up for dessert and then asked them for money. That would make my skin crawl.

After some social time I'd get up and basically preach a sermon based on the story of Jonathan attacking the Philistines, and I'd explain why we were launching a new church, why we had chosen the specific location, the details of how the finances would work, and I'd ask them to get involved financially. But along the way, I was trying to sell them on who I was. I knew that if this church was to succeed that it had to have solid preaching. So I wanted to demonstrate in the fundraising that I was a good enough preacher that if they gave, it would be money well spent.

After I was finished preaching I'd explain we were going to have some more social time during which they could grab some more dessert, and I'd make myself available for questions. I also explained that on their way out someone would give them a letter to recap what I had said and it contained a commitment form for them to give to our project. And it worked! We received more in commitments and gifts than we had even hoped.

So be yourself. If you are great one-on-one, schedule a hundred lunches. If you are great in front of a crowd, put yourself in front of a crowd. If you are the world's best writer, then write fundraising letters. But don't do or not do something just because "that's what you're supposed to do." Recognize your gifts and passions, and use them in fundraising. But even being yourself, there are some things you must do on the front end and on the back end to make fundraising a complete success.

***

Which of these is false?

- I played college basketball at a Division I school that I led to the Final Four. During college, I spent one semester studying at Oxford. After college, I did a stint at NASA where I worked on the space shuttle. Then I devoted myself to triathlons, even winning an Ironman. Since then I settled into a lifestyle of spending a third of my year in New York, a third in London, and a third in Miami.
- I played college basketball at a tiny school in a division called NCCAA, Division II, where I was the assist leader on our team. During college, I spent a summer working for FedEx. After college, I did a stint at a church plant that exploded after I got there. Then I devoted myself to marathons, where I broke three hours on my second try. Since then I've settled down in Maryland with my wife and 5 kids.

Did you figure out which is a lie?

They both are! I definitely didn't lead anyone to the final four, have never visited Oxford or attempted an Ironman. But I also was never an assist leader. I worked at

UPS, not FedEx; the church plant I worked at actually went down in attendance after I arrived as an intern; my second marathon I couldn't even break four hours, let alone three; and I am not brave enough to have five kids, just four.

The best lies that Satan tells us are not the ones that are one percent true. The best lies are 99 percent true, and that's why they're so believable. If you exaggerate your weight by 25 pounds someone will notice. If you exaggerate by five pounds, they probably won't. But they're both lies.

> # The worst lies are the lies we tell to ourselves.

As a pastor I often see this in relationships: "I deserved it." "He'll change." "I deserve better." But in church plant circles I actually see this in how we raise funds. So if you'll indulge me, here are the 3 most common lies we tell ourselves about fundraising:

Lie #1: "We'll learn to live below our means."

What is it going to cost to launch the type of church that is in your head? This gets back to the "What's your plan" question from chapter one. Living below your means is sound biblical wisdom. Every financial counselor teaches it. The problem is that some church planters don't take the time necessary to figure out exactly how much funding they need to launch. So you set about your fundraising and vision casting, which you're great at. But the reality is you don't know how much money it actually takes to fund your vision. So you are counting on God to overcome your lack of attention to detail. Even if you work extremely hard at fundraising, if you don't know exactly what it will cost to fund your church, you will always be living outside your means.

In addition, I believe by not figuring out what it will cost to launch, you are selling God short. Think about it: if you have a specific goal of money you are praying for and God gives that amount of money, then you can praise him for answering your need. But if you just say, "God, give us whatever you want," you can't really praise him because 1) you won't know when he's answered that and 2) you're not asking in faith anyway.

If you are not figuring out what your church plant costs, it demonstrates a lack of faith in God to provide and a lack of wisdom to be a good steward. I found in our fundraising that a handful of people were very interested in how we came up with our budget. And when I met those people I'd pull out the spreadsheet and show them line-by-line how this money would be spent. When that happened, those people felt reassured in their giving because they knew it was going to a specific plan and wouldn't be wasted because there wasn't a plan in place.

Lie #2: "God will provide the funds for this vision."

On the surface, who wouldn't agree with this statement? It is very biblical and sounds faith-based. And in the right context, I agree. But the contrarian church planter recognizes that this could be a façade for people to hide behind who don't want to act wisely or who God is calling not to plant.

Once you have figured out what you need to raise to make this new church a reality, then go raise your funds. And as fundraising is happening, it should be a validation of the vision. Unfortunately, some people believe that God wants them to plant in spite of having proper funding, so they push through with the vision when it is clear the funds aren't there.

So you have to ask the big Why. Why should people give to this project? (Or maybe, why *aren't* people giving to this project?)

When people aren't giving to your new church, it may be that you haven't been yourself or you haven't had a detailed enough budget or you haven't asked enough people yet. And it may be that fundraising is coming just a little short, in which case you need to re-adjust your budget to see if it will work.

But too many church planters have pushed through a vision that they couldn't raise money for and they end up with an unhealthy church and a failed vision, at best. (And sometimes a miserable marriage and a broken relationship with God at worst.)

Just a few miles from me is a church building that looks pretty impressive. Well, it *would* look impressive to me if it were finished. Obvious to everyone who drives by, this church began building a huge, multi-million dollar building on an expensive piece of property, but then they ran out of money. The parts that are finished look fantastic, but then you see plywood instead of a door, missing sidewalks, lack of pavement, wires hanging where lights should be, and it becomes obvious that their vision was bigger than their wallet.

It's been said that our vision should drive our budget, and that is true. But we must recognize that if there is no budget, God may be telling us No or he may be telling us to wait for that particular vision.

I would love for Mosaic to have a much larger impact than we currently do. I envision more campuses all over Maryland. I envision starting more churches on the East Coast. I envision sending church planters all over the world. And we have started to do those things in small ways. But the reality is that we can't afford to do all of those things full-scale right now. Does that mean the vision is wrong? Possibly. Does it mean it's wrong for right now? Yes. Don't be the person Jesus talks about in Luke 14 who builds a building but doesn't have enough money to finish it. That's what happened with the church around the corner from me, and it's given the entire church in Maryland a bit of a black eye.

Lie #3: We will become self-supportive.

Who are you going to reach and what will they give?

I really like impressionist paintings. If I have a free afternoon (and a babysitter), I love to spend several hours walking around the National Gallery of Art in Washington D.C. My favorite section, possibly because it's very extensive, is the impressionist gallery. The Manets, Renoirs, and Monets are beautiful, captivating, and tranquil. Once when I was there I was even able to jump on a tour explaining the unique intricacies of these paintings.

Impressionism, of course, is famous for its unique style. It began with a work of Monet's called, you guessed it, "impression." He saw a sunset, painted it, and gave a movement a name. Impressionists use larger brushstrokes and even globs of paint at times at the expense of clear delineation between things. They want to give, obviously, their impression of the subject matter more so than the exact detail of it, and it's that aspect to the art that makes it so compelling. Our minds can often find deeper meaning in something that is intentionally blurred.

The reason I bring up impressionism is that it's a great way for artists to view painting, but it's a terrible way for church planters to view their future offerings. One of the great things about church planting is the opportunity to reach niche markets. Bill Clinton's campaign manager became famous for breaking down the United States into various segments and tailoring a unique message to each segment. *Microtrends* explains that there are huge portions of the country that need a direct message or you won't reach them.

Church planters are on the cutting edge of this, as I've seen church plants targeted to homeless people, bikers, truckers, movie producers, military personnel, and even strippers. And the list could go on! That's fantastic, and I'm thankful so many churches are aiming to reach so many people. So when it comes to fundraising we must figure out how this will work long term. Too many planters flippantly say, "We will become self-supportive," without examining how that will happen. The questions I want to know include how many people will come and how much will they give per capita?

It may be unwise to say you will become self-supportive if your target is people who hate church and have lost their jobs in the last six months. Those people need Jesus, but they sure aren't going to fund a church.

We have to be realistic. Ideally, every local church becomes self-supportive. There are examples of churches in the Bible helping each other out in a time of great need, but the impression we get is not that the outside support was forever.

Know who you are going to reach and fundraise appropriately. If you come back to your supporters in year two looking for more money and say, "Well, it costs a lot more than we planned to reach people who hate church and are jobless," you're going to look like a bad leader. That does not inspire confidence…or giving.

Lie #4: I can move on from fundraising.

Middle school boys are some of the most unique creatures on earth. They stink, they look and talk funny, they are insecure, and do they ever need Jesus. I personally refer to middle school ministry as "purgatory," where you must pay for your sins.

My youth minister used to say that to keep the attention of teenage boys you just had to talk about two things: animals or bodily functions. If you talked about either of those things you'd keep a teenage boy's attention forever; leave those topics and lose his attention. It was in middle school that the fart joke became funny. By "the fart joke" I mean, "anything at all related to, sounding like, or smelling like a gas leaving your body." Pretending someone had farted, making fart noises, using a whoopee cushion, and anything related to farting was hilarious in middle school.

But in high school some of the jokes got old, so I thought, "I need to move on from this fart humor; that's middle school stuff." But when I went to college, you know what was always funny—or at least so stupid that it became funny? Fart humor. When I was out of college you know what my buddies and I thought was funny? Fart humor.

I know I'm grossing all the ladies out, so for all the females let me pull you in on a little secret: all males think farts are funny for the entire lives. They never "move on" from this. I'm convinced that when my buddies and I are in the nursing home someone will let one rip and we'll all crack up (#punintended).

And fundraising is just like fart jokes. Yes, I did just write that sentence. (My editor wanted to cut it, but I wouldn't let him.)

I did not like fundraising. God blessed our efforts so that we were very successful at it, but it's not something I cherished doing. So once we had completed the fundraising for our church plant I breathed a big sigh of relief and thanked God that was over. Boy, was I wrong. Because then I wanted to hire more staff, which meant more fundraising. Then I wanted to buy a cool portable baptistry. More fundraising. Then I wanted our church to move into a permanent facility from the movie theatre. More fundraising. Then I wanted us to have a live webcast that wasn't in the budget. Even more fundraising.

In retrospect, it seems perfectly clear that fundraising would be a never-ending job. And although the common wisdom says to keep fundraising, the common practice is to do it, complete it, and stop it, the contrarian church planter knows that fundraising is ongoing. I got two letters just last month asking for funds for new churches. The first explained why they needed the funds: several supporters had dropped off, their offerings were low, and so they needed more money. They did throw in at the end that they've baptized several dozen people in the last year.

The second letter told success story after success story, and it had actual names and stories listed. So as I read that letter, it wasn't a "give to us or we're out of business" appeal. It was more of them wanting me to relate to and know the people they were ministering to. What motivates me to give isn't the need or a blanket statement of success; it's a story.

So every month we were on support, we'd send our supporters a letter that told the story of one person they've impacted. It puts a name and puts emotion with where their dollars are going. And over and over they tell us the stories are why they keep giving. Today our attendees finance 100 percent of the ministry, and we still do the same thing: every quarter we send out a giving statement, telling a story of life change. And at the end of the year for several years we've sent out an annual report that shows numbers, but more importantly, tells stories.

***

My palms were sweaty, my heart racing. I tried to stay distracted as the team in the next room deliberated how much they would give to our new church. The hope was they would be our cornerstone partner. I knew they wouldn't give what we'd asked because I purposefully overshot. But if they didn't come anywhere close to what I'd asked we'd be in trouble.

The phone rang and the asked me to come back in.

I sat down, hands still moist. They were still sharing some small talk about golf and business. One of them finally said, "Carl, we're not going to give you what you asked." Okay. I was prepared for this. Just please be close, *please* be close.

He went on, "We're going to give you $29,000 *more* than what you asked."

What? Who—why? Huh?

He said, "Carl, we believe in you and what you're doing!"

I stammered out some thank you and shook their hands, and the meeting was over. Somehow in my shocked daze, I wandered into the sanctuary, and as I sat in this empty room I stared at the cross, thanking God for his faithfulness. We had implemented some good fundraising principles, but only God could plan what had just happened. And for your church, only God owns the cattle on a thousand hills. But he asks us to walk wisely. So...

- Know how much you need to raise.
- Raise ALL the money it's going to take.
- Come up with a plan to be self-supportive.
- Keep fundraising by telling the stories.

If you can do these four things you are setting yourself up for success in church planting, at least financially. However, next I'll explain why, if you do things the normal way, your church will never reach its maximum potential impact.

Chapter 4

BE WHO YOU WANT TO BE

Kevin Kelley is a freak. And I love him.

Unless you've read *Scorecasting* you've probably never heard of Kevin Kelley, so I'll introduce you. Kevin is the head football coach at Pulaski Academy in Little Rock, Arkansas. The methods he employs as a coach have gotten this 350-person school to win five high school state championships in his twelve seasons and ranked in the top 100 high schools nationally. So what's his secret that has turned this tiny school into a Goliath in high school football? Kelley's team doesn't kick the ball. Ever. No extra points, no punting, no kickoffs. When kicking off they do an onside kick—every time. In a recent game highlighted by *Sports Illustrated*, they were playing a big game in front of 8,000 people with the local news broadcasting live from the game. What happened? Pulaski

Academy got up 29-0 *before the other team even touched the ball.*

His fans refer to Kelley as the "mad scientist," but really he's perfectly rational. See, he has run the numbers and has realized that mathematically, kicking *decreases* his chances of winning. So he doesn't do it, ever.

From *Scorecasting:*

"According to Kelley's statistics, when a team punts from...deep, the opponent will take possession inside the 40-yard line and, from such a favorable distance, will score a touchdown 77 percent of the time. Meanwhile, if the fourth-down attempt is unsuccessful and the opponent recovers on downs inside the 10-yard line, it will score a touchdown 92 percent of the time. So [by forsaking] a punt you give your offense a chance to stay on the field. And if you miss, the odds of the other team scoring a touchdown [only] increase 15 percent."

And that's just the beginning. Kelley knows the state high school stats for average fourth down conversions, average punt, average kickoff return, average yards per running and passing play, and pretty much anything else that influences whether or not you should go for it on fourth down. It's been two years since one of his teams punted, and that was just because his team was up by so much he didn't want to score. (The irony? The other team ran it back for a touchdown, further cementing Kelley's belief that punting is detrimental to a high school team's chances of winning.)

The reason I love Kevin Kelley is that he is both completely rational and completely insane at the same time. He is rational because every decision he makes on what play to run is based on the math. The numbers don't lie, you can't manipulate the data, and ultimately the numbers (on the scoreboard) determine the champion. But he is also completely insane. Not literally of course. But in football, everyone knows you have to kick sometimes. Sometimes it's just better to punt away or kick it off deep.

And everyone's wrong.

I think Kevin Kelley would be a good church planter. Because too many churches do it like it's always been done before. We read in church books that the worst phrase to say is "We've never done it that way before!" So church planters have a tendency to go to the opposite extreme. We say I'll do it like it's never been done before.

As an example, think of the names of churches. It seems every church plant wants to have a name that no other church has ever had. So there's Guts Church, the Homeless Church, and Urban Refuge. I've heard of "The Ascent"—is that a mountain climbing club or a church?

New churches are into points. There is NorthPointe, CenterPoint, Ocean Point, Life Point, Bridge Point, Faith Point and Midpoint. Of course, you have the biblical-language-churches: Ekklesia, Scum of the Earth, and Jacob's Well. There are the churches that are into motion: Momentum, Velocity, and Kinetic.

We named our church Mosaic, and I'll admit, we wanted something with a cool metaphor, even if it wasn't 100 percent original.[1]

One friend told me he was naming his church plant *Paradox Church*. I asked what that meant and he said, "Exactly!" I guess I'm not smart enough because I still don't get it.

Another friend of mine named his church plant *Just Church*. That's it. Just...*Just Church*. Sounds like low self-image to me. What's special about your church. "Nuthin...we're just church."

I'm making fun here, but I think since I've done the same thing I'm allowed. My point is that we as church planters spend a lot of energy trying to be different, and while there's nothing wrong with that, we have to be careful about being different for difference's sake.

The Conventional Practice Is to Do It Like Never Before

We see this in our names, our strategy, even how we offend people.

Have you ever heard of the Me Monster? Comedian Brian Regan talks about the Me Monster, how if you're at a dinner party there's always someone ready to story-top you. Regan says he made the mistake once of mentioning he got two wisdom teeth taken out. But as soon as he

---

[1] However, I was really confused the first time I took a call from someone with questions about our church and she asked if we worshiped Moses. Umm, what? "You know, because it's called *Mosaic*, I thought your church would be into the Mosaic Law." Ohhh, umm, no. We just think mosaics are cool and a great picture of what God wants to do with the broken pieces of our lives. "Ohhhh." She never came.

finished someone interrupted, "That ain't nuthin!" And he proceeded to tell about how he had four wisdom teeth taken out, they were impacted, and the roots were like trees wrapped around their jawbone. Regan recommends, "Never tell a two-wisdom teeth tale." Then he adds, "That's why I'd like to be one of the twelve men who have walked on the moon. Because you can just sit back and let all the Me Monsters tell their stories about how great they are…and you just casually add between bites, "Yeah, well….I walked on the moon." Boom! Ain't nobody gonna top that one!

As church planters, we must beware of the Me Monster, of wanting to make a name for ourselves because we know how to do it like it's never been done before.

Have you ever heard someone give an awkward testimony? I don't mean awkward because they're not good at sharing in public; I'm referring to the person who is telling about how they came to Christ, but as they go into detail about the sin Christ saved them from, you're not sure if they are really repentant, because it sounds like they would love to go back to that sin at a moment's notice? With testimonies, there can be a fine line between being proud of your sin and being proud of the one who saved you from sin.

Similarly, in church planting, there is a fine line between being different to reach new people with the Gospel and being different for difference's sake. See, a lot of church planters saw a church that was ineffective because it used the deadly phrase, "We've never done it that way before." That phrase is uttered by churches on a hamster-wheel-death-march to obscurity and irrelevance. So the church planter's temptation is to do the opposite, to say, "We've never done it that way before…so we *must* do it that way!"

> # The contrarian does what will best reach people, whether it's been done that way before or not.

I'm convinced that if King David had been a church planter, he would've fit this description. David, as we know, was a man after God's own heart. But David was himself. He wrote much of my favorite Scriptures, the Psalms. Recently I read Psalm 59 again and I know I've read it before but I must have scanned it too quickly because I never picked up on something until recently.

The first part of this Psalm he praises God and explains that people are trying to assassinate him. In verse 11 he asks God not to kill his enemies and I'm thinking, "That's nice of David because Jesus later says to love your enemies and David is asking God not to kill these people who are trying to kill him." Wrong. Because David proceeds to explain:

> *God, I want you to keep them alive so you can torture them and cause them as much pain as you possibly can, all in view of as many people as*

possible—just to show what happens when people
oppose the righteous. In fact, God, can you go Jack
Bauer on them and electrocute them, pluck out their
eyebrows one by one, shoot them in areas that
won't kill them, and take them just to the brink of
death so they can suffer. (Personal paraphrase.)

We read this and think, "Holy crap! David needs to lighten up! Show a little grace, man!" But consider: maybe the reason David was a man after God's heart wasn't because he was perfect, as he obviously wasn't. Maybe the reason God loved David's heart is that it was completely honest and open before God.

The best story of David being himself is in 2 Samuel 6. You remember the story: David had just become king, he defeats the Philistines, and they bring the ark of God into Jerusalem. This represented the presence of God coming back to reside in Israel. So as part of the impromptu parade, David sheds his clothes and dances in his underwear before God.

And this is just my opinion, but here's my guess....I think David was a *terrible* dancer. I do! It just fits the context of the story. If David's a great dancer, everyone's impressed and it's just one more great thing David does. His wife Michal wouldn't have been nearly embarrassed if he was someone who should be on *So You Think You Can Dance?* Here's why I believe David was a terrible dancer: the story says he danced before God "with all his might."

Have you ever seen someone dance with all their might? It's not a good scene. A great dancer looks effortless, they're fluid, it's beautiful. When someone dances with all their might they're…well, they're Jody Otte.

Jody is one of the most unique people I've ever met. He's probably the smartest person I know, as well as a dapper dresser and the life of the party. I don't know if you remember Ska music, but Jody loved it, and he had turned Ska dancing into its own art form. I am not sure what he was doing was actually called "dancing," but there was music and he was moving, so I think that's what it was supposed to be. But Jody definitely danced with all his might. You get him on the dance floor for just a couple songs, and he would move so vigorously he needed to wring out his clothes of sweat. In addition, he had a constant expression while dancing that was something between a lackadaisical attitude, violent anger, and constipation. And of course, he had the same problem that all bad dancers have: he loved to dance! We loved watching Jody dance because it was a hilarious spectacle every time. But here's the thing: we could laugh in Jody's face, and you know how much he cared? Not at all. Nada. Zilch. He was going to have a good time, and on the dance floor, no one could deter him.

I think David was like Jody. If he were dancing with all his might, that's code for "he looked like a fool, everyone laughed at him, but he didn't even care." In fact, when his wife Michal berates him for acting like a fool, I'm pretty confident that it's not just because he was in his underwear; it was also his dancing.

But David didn't care if he looked like a fool, and neither should we. We, therefore, have to ask ourselves two important questions about ourselves.

Question #1: Are you willing to be yourself if it means foolishly being different from everyone else?

David knew that God wanted his worship, so he worshiped God with all his energy, sacrificing his pride in the process. He didn't care what anyone thought—he just wanted God to know David loved him. Are you willing to be like David?

Here's the irony about Kevin Kelley's story. Even though the math is on his side when it comes to always going for two and refusing to punt, no one else does it. There are a few outliers at lower levels of football who are intrigued and want to learn from him. But when you make the jump to the NFL, no one does his style, even though the math still says he's right. In fact, Cal-Berkeley economist David Romer published a study on NFL game theory that showed, among other things, that "regardless of field position, on anything less than fourth and five, teams are *always* better off going for it." Romer observed 1068 fourth-down situations in which statistics say the right decision is to go for it, yet the NFL teams punted 959 of those times.

Why? If NFL coaches are paid millions of dollars to win, why do they make decisions that give them a *worse* chance of winning?

Peer pressure.

If a coach goes for it on fourth down in his own territory (cough, cough, Bill Belichick) and doesn't get it and loses the game, the analyst shows will bash him all week. But if he gets the first down he doesn't get near the amount of praise as he would criticism.

The connection to church planting is obvious, right? Sometimes the right thing to do is what everyone else thinks is the wrong thing. You're going to reach *those* people? Your services will be *where? What* are you preaching on? Has that strategy worked *anywhere* before? I've never heard of a church doing *that* kind of outreach before.

A good test of if you are willing to be yourself is if you are willing to receive criticism. Jesus could have avoided a lot of criticism if he had just acted like everyone else. He was criticized for being a drunk, hanging out with prostitutes, and bashing the establishment. If we are following the leading of Jesus, should we expect to be any different?

Sometimes I'll start to feel sorry for myself when I receive criticism about our church's style or audience or vision or advertising. And I think the reason it stings is that it often comes from well-meaning Christians. But I have to remind myself that this is what I signed up for. And if I don't want to be criticized I'd better stop following Jesus, stop being myself, and stop being different from everyone else.

Now honestly, it's pretty easy most of the time for church planters to answer a resounding Yes to question #1. You're planting a church, which is a huge risk already, so starting a new ministry, strategy or tactic isn't necessarily the most difficult thing. And that's why question two is so essential. It highlights our motives and asks if have true humility.

Question #2: Are you willing to be yourself if it means acting like everyone expects you to act?

Most of the time David did what a king is supposed to do. Right before this story and right after this story we read of David winning military victories. He defeats the enemy, defends the homeland, and provides security to his nation. I'm sure these battles were more interesting than the few sentences written about them, but the bottom line is he was doing what everyone in the country hoped—and expected—he would do. He didn't go dancing in his underwear every single day.

Sometimes being yourself, being who you think you should be, means being exactly who other people think you should be as well. As church planters, we resist this at times because we want to be different, we want to blaze a new trail, but sometimes things have been done a certain way because that's the best way to do things.

James Surowiecki, in his book *The Wisdom of Crowds*, demonstrates that often a crowd knows better than any individual. He kicks off the book by telling the story of British scientist Francis Galton.

In 1906 Galton attended the West England Fat Stock and Poultry Exhibition. At the exhibition, Galton came across a crowd lining up to place wagers on the weight of an ox. You could pay to enter your guess, and the person who was closest won a prize. Eight hundred people tried their luck. Some were experts like farmers and butchers. Others had no idea what they were guessing: clerks and students, for example.

Galton wanted to see how foolish the average mind is, so after the contest, he asked for and was given all the tickets that showed people's guesses. He arranged them all in order and figured out the average. What he found astounded him. The average guess of the crowd from the exhibition was that the ox would weigh 1,197 pounds.

The actual weight of the ox? 1,198 pounds.

Surowiecki concludes: "In other words, the crowd's judgment was essentially perfect."

Sometimes we need to go along with the crowd because that's the best way to do things. Let me use dating to illustrate the biggest way this needs to be true.

Have you ever had a friend who was embarrassed about his girlfriend? You see him hanging out with a particular girl and ask if they're dating and he says, "Oh, noooo man, sick, no way!" You shrug it off but the next week you hear they went to dinner and a movie over the weekend, so you ask again. The response is even more vehement than before: "No wayyy man! I'd never go out with her!" You point out that actions speak louder than words, but he rolls his eyes and walks off. If this goes on much longer you will inevitably conclude two things: first, they are indeed dating. Second, he is ashamed to admit it!

Here's an unfortunate truth about church planters: sometimes we're ashamed to be grouped with other pastors and churches. We want to be known as the ones who are different, the ones blazing new trails, the ones who really understand what it takes to reach people.

But let's call it what it is: pride. It's pride that forces me to come up with a new style of doing ministry just because. It's pride that makes me roll my eyes at an outreach idea that's been around 30 years. It's pride that makes fun of churches with a different dress code. It's pride that prevents me from borrowing sermon ideas from other preachers.

And the scary thing about pride is that it separates me from Jesus. When I start thinking prideful thoughts I turn right into the Pharisee from Luke 18. As horrible as this is, I have literally said before, "God, thank you that I'm not irrelevant like that church/pastor/etc." But Jesus warns, "Those who exalt themselves will be humbled, but those who humble themselves will be exalted."

Pastors, being contrarian does not mean being filled with pride. It means doing whatever it takes to accomplish the mission of seeking and saving the lost. Sometimes that will mean doing what has never been done before. Sometimes that will mean doing what's been done a thousand times before. We are made in the image of a creative God, so God doesn't want us to fit into the mold without thinking. But are we proudly blazing new trails, or are we dedicated to the search and rescue mission that is God's church so we can bring God's lost children home?

Warning Label

I don't know if you've seen these commercials they've had lately on TV. They'll do a commercial for some new pharmaceutical product, a new drug they've come out with. They paint this wonderful picture of this drug. Music will be playing, people will be laughing and running through fields all because of this wonderful new drug. Then at the end of the commercial, they quickly list the side effects. I guess they're required by law to do this. Often times the side effects seem worse than the illness the drug is supposed to relieve. I read one article that listed the side effects of a hypothetical drug. The instructions said to take two tablets every six hours for joint pain. Now listen to the side effects:

SIDE EFFECTS: *This drug may cause joint pain, nausea, headache, or shortness of breath. You may also experience muscle aches, rapid heartbeat, impotence and ringing in the ears. If you feel faint, call your doctor. Do not consume alcohol while taking this pill; likewise, avoid red meat, shellfish, and vegetables. Approved foods: Flounder. Leg cramps are to be expected; if bowel movements become greater than 12 per hour, consult your doctor. You may find yourself becoming lost or vague; may cause stigmata in Ukrainians. May induce a tendency to compulsively repeat the phrase "no can do." You may feel a powerful sense of impending doom. Do not take this product if you are uneasy with lockjaw you also may experience a growing dissatisfaction with life along with a deep sense of melancholy. WARNING: This drug may shorten your intestines by 21 feet. Has been known to cause birth defects in the user retroactively. Women experience a lowering of the voice, an increase in ankle hair. Sensations of levitation are illusory, as is the sensation of having a "phantom" third arm. Twenty minutes after taking the pills, you will feel an insatiable craving to take another dose. AVOID THIS WITH ALL YOUR POWER.*

This chapter of being who you want to be needs a warning label. It doesn't have anything about intestines or flounder, but there are 2 dangers here.

Warning #1: It's easy to go to one extreme or the other

Most often church planters gravitate to one side or the other. They will either do everything differently than everyone else, or they'll do everything the same as everyone else. Both extremes are bad because both are fitting into a mold. The person who grows up saying, "I'll never be like my dad," is still controlled by his father. Being yourself requires wisdom, discipline, and creativity. Most of all, it takes hard work. It's easier to put things on cruise control and go with a certain flow. It takes work to figure out what you need to do differently and what you need to simply adopt from others.

Warning #2: It's easy to start off with a good balance but then drift toward one extreme or the other

I have a friend who recently got hired on as a firefighter. He was really excited because he had trained well, studied hard, and finally attained his dream job. During his training, he was working out all the time to stay in shape in order to pass all the physical fitness tests that were required of him. But I recently learned the number one killer of firefighters in our nation. Do you know what it is? It's not smoke inhalation. That's what it was in the 1970s and 80s.

The number one cause of death on the job for firefighters in the United States is heart failure. More firefighters die because they are out of shape than die from inadequate equipment, bad training, or accidents. They worked hard to be in shape to get the job, but once they got the job, many let themselves go. For some, it has drastic consequences.

Our tendency as church planters is to look at Question 1 and say, "Of course! Of course I'm willing to buck the trends. I'm starting a church, aren't I?" And it's true: if you're willing to take the risk of planting a new church then you *are* willing to take risks and be different.

> # We must never lose the risk-taking mentality that got us to where we are now.

On a dangerous seacoast where shipwrecks often occur, some people banded together to create a little life-saving station. The building was primitive, and there was just one boat, but the members of the life-saving station were committed and kept a constant watch over the sea. When a ship went down, they braved the waters day or night to save those in peril. Because so many lives were saved by that station, it became famous. Consequently, many people wanted to be associated with the station to give their time, talent, and money to support its important work. New boats were bought, new crews were recruited, and a formal training session was offered. As the crew of the life-saving station grew in numbers, some became unhappy that the building was so primitive and that the equipment was so outdated. They wanted a better place to welcome the survivors pulled from the sea. So they replaced the emergency cots with beds and put better furniture in the enlarged and newly decorated building.

Now the life-saving station became a popular gathering place. People met regularly there, and it was apparent how they loved being together. They greeted each other, hugged each other, and shared with one another the events that had been going on in their lives. But fewer members were now interested in going to sea on life-saving missions; so they hired lifeboat crews to do this for them. About this time, a large ship was wrecked off of the coast, and the hired crews brought into the life-saving station boatloads of cold, wet, dirty, sick, and half-drowned people. Some of them had black skin, and some had yellow skin. Some could speak English well, and some could hardly speak it at all. Some were first-class cabin passengers of the ship, and some were the deckhands. The beautiful meeting place became a place of chaos. The plush carpets got dirty. Some of the exquisite furniture got scratched. So the property committee immediately had a shower built outside the house where the victims of shipwreck could be cleaned up before coming inside.

At the next meeting, there was a rift in the membership. Most of the members wanted to stop the club's life-saving activities, for they were unpleasant and a hindrance to the normal fellowship of the members. Other members insisted that life-saving was their primary purpose and pointed out that they were still called a life-saving station. But they were finally voted down and told that if they wanted to save the lives of all those various kinds of people who would be shipwrecked, they could begin their own life-saving station down the coast. And do you know what? That is what they did.

As the years passed, the new station experienced the same changes that had occurred in the old. It evolved into a place to meet regularly for fellowship, for committee meetings, and for special training sessions about their mission, but few went out to the drowning people. The drowning people were no longer welcomed in that new life-saving station. So another life-saving station was founded further down the coast. History continued to repeat itself. And if you visit that seacoast today, you will find a number of adequate meeting places with ample parking and plush carpeting. Shipwrecks are frequent in those waters, but most of the people drown.

***

You have been called to join Jesus' mission of seeking and saving the lost. God wants to use your unique personality and gifts to do this. So you must wisely choose whatever will best reach people, whether it's been done that way before or not. However, you won't be who you want to be if you buy into the biggest self-help myth today, which is what we'll talk about next.

Chapter 5

THE MYTH OF THE BALANCED LIFE

Our church was two months from launching, our launch team was declining in number, I had gained 25 pounds, I was taking sleeping pills, and I thought I should be dusting off my résumé.

Been there? I thought you might have.

In every church plant there comes a time (many times, probably) where there just aren't enough hours in the day, not enough days in the week, to do everything that needs to be done. In my story, I went to our regularly scheduled management team meeting and confessed, "I don't know what to do. I feel like I'm cheating everything. I'm not giving enough time to the church, I'm not giving enough time to my family, I'm not giving enough time to my exercise or sleep or eating or spiritual disciplines or...anything!"

I was trying to do what conventional wisdom said I needed to do: live a balanced life. There was only one problem with that.

The balanced life is a myth.

As a church planter, you are about as likely to discover a unicorn, meet a leprechaun, or see the Browns win the Super Bowl as you are to have a balanced life.

There are plenty of people who disagree with that. In fact, most of my life I was taught by books, seminars, teachers, and preachers that I could live a balanced life. We imagine a tightrope walker carefully taking one step in front of the other and we compare our hectic lives and competing priorities and think, "If I could balance everything as well as he's balanced on that wire I would be successful." But unlike the tightrope walker, we seem to fall down over and over again. The contrarian church planter recognizes this and gives up trying to achieve the myth of the balanced life.

Think about it: the Bible says nothing about living a balanced life. I don't find much in the Bible that says our spiritual disciplines should be balanced. Yes, Jesus teaches us to pray for our daily bread. Yes, the king was supposed to keep a copy of the Old Testament law nearby to read it frequently. However, the 15-minute daily quiet time is not in the Bible.

I don't see much in the Bible that describes our handling of money as balanced. There are many times in the Bible where people are irrationally generous, which screams "imbalance."

I don't see much in the Bible that describes following Jesus as balanced. Jesus says if you want to follow him to pick up your cross. To a man who wants to bury his parents Jesus waves him off and says, "Eh, if you put your hand to the plow but look back you're not fit to follow me." (That's from the CET—Carl's Everyday Translation.) He says to a rich man to sell everything and then come and follow Jesus…not very balanced.

And outside the Bible, we can observe pretty quickly that balance doesn't work. Think about some common activities:

- If you train for a marathon, you are out of balance physically. No one needs to run 20, 40, or more miles per week to be in shape.
- If you have a baby, you are out of balance towards your family. You don't get enough sleep for months so you can feed and rock that baby, you neglect other relationships because the baby has to have her nap time and be on schedule, and you sacrifice lots of money to buy every baby product under the sun.
- If you go on vacation you are out of balance towards relaxing. No one needs to sit on the deck of a cruise ship for a week straight and do nothing but get a tan, gain ten pounds at the buffet, and get ripped off at each port's shopping area.

And if you plant a church, you are out of balance towards the church. It seems insane to work seventy, eighty, ninety hours per week for the church. When that begins to happen, as church planters we have a few different reactions.

Some people believe it's unhealthy and cap it at forty hours per week, no matter how the church is going or what needs to get done. Some planters assume that's what is required of pastors, so they settle into that schedule for their entire careers. But the contrarian church planter recognizes both its insanity and its need. And knows there must be a third way.

So what to do?

> # The contrarian's practice is to choose your imbalance wisely.

Stephen Covey, the author of *The Seven Habits of Highly Effective People,* wrote, "the essence of effective time and life management is to organize and execute around priorities." The contrarian recognizes this and uses wisdom as the filter through which to figure out his priorities. Ephesians 5:15-16 says, "Be very careful, then, how you live—not as unwise but as wise, making the most of every opportunity, because the days are evil."

The contrarian planter uses wisdom as a filter to understand how to be imbalanced. Let's go back to the image of the tightrope walker because I think we focus on the wrong thing and miss the more profound lesson.

***

My favorite tightrope walker is Philippe Petit. You may have seen his story in the documentary *Man on Wire*. Philippe became famous for his most daring walk, which took place on August 7, 1974.

Petit was at a doctor's office in France in the 1960s when he read an article on the yet-to-be-constructed Twin Towers of the World Trade Center. From that point, he became obsessed with walking a tightrope between the two extraordinarily tall buildings. After years of planning and practice, on August 6, 1974, Petit and his crew snuck into the 2 towers and ascended the 104 floors to the roof. To string a wire between the towers they used a bow and arrow to first shoot a fishing line across. Then they pulled across progressively heavier lines until they could string across the steel wire, securing it to each tower.

At 7:15 am the next day, Philippe Petit stepped out from the security of the tower to a wire that dangled 1368 feet above the streets below. People on the street stopped and pointed. Some smiled. Others gasped. All were captivated.

As you can imagine, the police were immediately called, but when they arrived at the roof just as Petit was about to complete the walk, he did the most surprising thing yet...he turned around! He walked back and forth eight times, but that wasn't all. He jumped up and down on the wire, he laid down on the wire (seeming to have a conversation with a bird that was quite interested in him), he danced, and he ran.

Finally, he gave himself up to police. (Ironically, when

the Port Authority realized all the free publicity for the towers this caused around the world, all charges were dropped.) And I love what Philippe had to say when asked about it afterward. He said: "To me, it's not courage; it's passion."

See, when we look at Philippe Petit we focus completely on the wrong metaphor. We want to know how he achieves that balance. For Petit, the story isn't about balance; it's about adventure. When Petit was asked about the possibility of death he said, "If I die, what a beautiful death!" What? Seriously? He's 1300 feet in the air, and he's thinking that if he dies it will be beautiful?

Yes, and that's exactly the point.

No tightrope walker ever says, "I'm proud I achieved perfect balance." Instead, the tightrope walker tries to achieve something no one else can do, to stare in the face of death and achieve something that gives those who watch sweaty palms and pits in their stomachs, to go to greater heights than most of us can imagine.

The point of tightrope walking isn't to achieve balance; it's to inspire others by achieving something they only dream about. That's why Petit says, "It's not courage; it's passion," because to him it's not something that he chose to do. In a sense, it's something that chose him.

The Balance of Passion

I have become convinced that we ask the wrong question. The question for us is not: How do we achieve balance in our lives? The question we should ask is: Will we live out our passion?

A friend of mine completed an Ironman triathlon a few

years ago. In case you've forgotten, an Ironman consists of a 2.4-mile swim, 112 miles on the bike, followed by an entire marathon: 26.2 miles. It is insane. You have seventeen hours to complete the 140 miles, but the championship-level athletes finish in around eight hours. My friend did it in eleven, which is pretty impressive for your first Ironman. When I talked to him about it, I was in awe of him, but he didn't seem to think it was that big of a deal. I pointed this out and his response was: "It's not that hard. *Anyone who has twenty hours a week can do an Ironman.*"

Umm, yeah, that would be the problem! Where am I going to get 20 hours per week to run, bike and swim? That's why he's an Ironman and why I'm a Chick-Fil-A man.

But he has hit on a key for all of us when it comes to balance and passion. We can have one or the other. If you live a perfectly balanced life you'll never achieve anything that requires more than minimum effort. In *Outliers*, Malcolm Gladwell wrote about the "10,000-hour rule". This is the idea that to achieve true greatness in a field you have to put in 10,000 hours of deliberate practice into it, whether the "it" is an instrument, science, or sport. Putting 10,000 hours into something isn't balance—it's passion.

Planting a church takes passion. One of my college professors said, "Don't go into ministry unless you can't do anything else." While I disagree with taking that statement literally, I do agree that it takes strong single mindedness. It takes passion to ask for more money after you've received yet another "no." It takes passion to move to a city where you don't know a single person. It takes passion to get people on board with your vision. It takes passion to stay true to the call when you are receiving criticism on every side. It takes passion to stay the course when you're launch team is dwindling while the launch day approaches.

Do you know where we get the word "passion"? It's from the Latin *passio* referring to the suffering of Jesus. Any time we use the word "passion" we're making an indirect reference to the brutal whipping, beating, and crucifixion of Jesus. And that's a great image because the last thing it took for Jesus to undergo that suffering was balance—it was his passion, it was his drive, it was his single-minded obsession that drove him to the cross.

How Do I Avoid Going Crazy?

This is an important question, right? If we're going to purposefully be out of balance at times, how do we avoid getting so out of balance that we go crazy because we're so obsessed?

Recognize imbalance towards unhealthy things.

There are many things that people are imbalanced towards today that are unhealthy. Many in our culture spend way too much time on social media, following their favorite sports team, playing the latest video game, watching as many movies as they can on Netflix, or even sleeping as much as they can.

> The reality is that you will live an imbalanced life. The question is simply, towards what?

Will it be something proactive like your family, getting in shape, and your church? Or will it be something passive like social media, the type of thing that you look at the clock and realize you wasted two hours of your life there? Be careful of an unhealthy imbalance.

I think this is actually why people talk about balance. They recognize they have a few sinful indulgences: food, Facebook, whatever. So they want to get "balanced" by sprinkling on a few good things: healthy eating, Bible reading, etc.

But wouldn't it be better to eliminate things that cause an unhealthy imbalance in our lives? If Dunkin Donuts is making you overweight, find a route to work that doesn't take you by it. If your newest video game is keeping you up late at night because you've got to play "just one more round", sell the game system. If Instagram borders on addiction, delete your account.

A friend of mine began his Ph.D. program a couple years ago and because he wanted to focus solely on the academics at hand, he chose not to get on Facebook until his Ph.D. was complete. He did make one exception, to show a picture of his first child! But the fact that he only broke his "Facebook fast" that one time shows where his focus and his priorities lay.

Practice the Rhythm of Sabbath

In the pre-launch stage of our church, my wife and I had a "state of the marriage" discussion. Specifically, we needed to get on the same page so that it was not just I who was choosing to be imbalanced in the church planting effort, but it was a joint decision. I was working an average of eighty hours per week those days, with some weeks much higher. When Lindsay and I talked about it there were two things she asked of me, mostly with our young daughter in mind: 1) take an entire day off each week, and 2) be home by five each day to help with our child.

Those were big sacrifices because the to-do list was never-ending. I trusted her wisdom though, so I accommodated. Being home at five meant that I had to start working a lot earlier. So every single day I was at work before my wife even got up, and believe me, she wasn't sleeping in.

I also had to learn to practice the Sabbath. I don't know if you've realized, but the Sabbath is pretty much the overlooked command of today. We rationalize that the Fourth Commandment isn't repeated explicitly as a command in the New Testament, and we don't want to be Pharisaic legalists, so we throw it out the window altogether. If an email needs to be answered on our day off, or a sermon needs touching up, or a phone call needs to be made, we make it happen.

But Jesus said that we *need* the Sabbath: The Sabbath was made to meet the needs of people, and not people to meet the requirements of the Sabbath. (Mark 2:27) For Type-A church planters, that's difficult to hear. We object with a series of "Yeah, buts."

Yeah, but what if my sermon's not finished? Yeah, but what if a volunteer cancels? Yeah, but what if I stayed up late trying to save someone's marriage? Yeah but, Yeah but, yeah but.

We care about the church, there's always something more to do, and it seems the church will be worse off if we take a day completely off. But practicing the rhythm of Sabbath is an act of humility. It's trusting God to do more with your six days than you can do with seven. This requires humility and it requires trust. But you see God's providence pay off in the end.

The Contrarian Church Planter needs a Sabbath. You will be so busy that you will burn out if you neglect this ancient practice. In fact, I think it goes beyond just one day per week. The Old Testament commanded seven different festivals for the Israelite people. These were times to celebrate God, but also to have a good time and stop working for a day or even a week. The modern equivalent for us, in a sense, is our vacations. One pastor I know says using all his vacation time is for him a spiritual discipline because without it he is not the best pastor, dad, and husband he should be.

One business where you don't take a day off is the restaurant business and if anyone could say, "Yeah, but," it's someone who owned a restaurant. But when Truett Cathy opened his first restaurant in 1946, he decided he would honor God and close every Sunday. Later as his business expanded he kept this principle, and today all 2,000 Chick-Fil-A restaurants in the country are closed on Sunday. Truett Cathy said about this: "Our decision to close on Sunday was our way of honoring God and directing our attention to things more important than our business. If it took seven days to make a living with a restaurant, then we needed to be in some other line of work. Through the years, I have never wavered from that position."

Here's the point: could Chick-Fil-A make money on Sundays? Yes. Does it seem like a good business decision to close on Sundays? No. But Chick-Fil-A continuously wins awards for best taste and best service, and as of several years ago, their sales-per-store were higher than McDonald's, Subway, Starbucks, Chipotle, and Panera. Truett Cathy said, "God, I believe you can do more with our six days than we can do with seven." And that's exactly what's happened.

Have a Lot of Sex

That's right. Have a lot of sex. (I told you this wasn't your typical church planting book.) A lot of Christians get tattoos of Bible verses, but for some reason, I've never seen anyone with a tattoo of 1 Corinthians 7:3-4. I doubt I have to remind you of what it says, but just in case:

"The husband should fulfill his marital duty to his wife, and likewise the wife to her husband. The wife does not have authority over her own body but yields it to her husband. In the same way, the husband does not have authority over his own body but yields it to his wife."

Carl's translation: "Once you're married you should have sex as much as possible." Then, paraphrasing the next section: "The only reason you should not have sex, according to the Bible, is to pray. But after you pray, have sex some more."

I'm not just saying this for the fun of it. There are two specific benefits of having a lot of sex. The first benefit is that it is a great stress reliever. As a church planter, you will likely experience more stress than at any point in your life. There are many things you can and should do to relieve this stress, but one of the best things you can do is to have sex.

This isn't just my opinion-this is science. A study recently examined participants' blood pressure to measure their stress while public speaking or performing challenging math problems. The researchers found that the participants who had recently had intercourse tended to have lower baseline blood pressures, less of a blood pressure rise during stressful events, or both. The summary stated: "These findings suggest that having sex can lead to less of a stress response during challenging situations, which is a good thing."

The other benefit to having a lot of sex is the benefit to your marriage. Consider these sobering statistics:

- According to Christianity Today, 40% of American pastors are addicted to pornography.
- Another study of pastors sponsored by Christianity Today found that 23% of 300 pastors admitted some

form of sexually inappropriate behavior with someone other than their wives while in the ministry.

- Bill Mitchell states that up to 5% of all affairs in the United States involve clergy.

A few weeks ago I read yet another resignation letter from a church planter who was caught in his sin and had to confess to his church the huge error he had made.

I'm not so naïve to think that there aren't deep issues sometimes related to an affair. But Proverbs gives a very simple prescription to avoid an affair:

Drink water from your own cistern, running water from your own well.
Should your spring overflow in the streets, your streams of water in the public square?
Let them be yours alone, never to be shared with strangers.
May your fountain be blessed, and may you rejoice in the wife of your youth.
A loving doe, a graceful deer—may her breasts satisfy you always, may you ever be intoxicated with her love.
Why, my son, be intoxicated with another man's wife? Why embrace the bosom of a wayward woman? (Proverbs 5:15-20)

The Bible says the way to avoid an affair is to have a lot of sex with your spouse!

Not only will that help to affair-proof your marriage, it

also makes your union stronger. When there are sexual arousal and release, a chemical called oxytocin is released in your brain. There is a strong bond that takes place when this chemical is released, so during sexual arousal and release, these chemicals are being released into our brain. And that's a wonderful thing if you're with your spouse because it's binding you to them. In a sense, it's addicting you to them.

I heard one pastor's wife encourage a group of pastors' wives: "Have sex with your husband as much as you can stand it!" I wasn't sure how to take that, to be honest! But I do know that when planting a church your temptation, exhaustion, and stress will be at all-time highs. One way to help that is to have a lot of sex.

Run, Forrest, Run

I opened the chapter by explaining to you my dilemma of feeling spent and cheating everything while giving my best to nothing. The conversation that ensued went something like this.

Me: I'm going and going and going!

Management Team: [blank stares]

Me: I'm cheating everything. I'm not sure what else to do.

Management Team: [blank stares]

Me: [blank stare]

[long pause.]

Person #1: You're a runner, right Carl?

Me: Well, I was before I planted a church. I'm not any longer!

Person #1: Why don't you start running again?

Me: Okay…anything else?

Person #2: Carl, you're planting a church! We expect this to be a hard time for you. So just run. And it'll help with the stress a little.

Me: [blank stare]

That was when I was still figuring out the balanced life was a myth. Fortunately, I had a wise team, and fortunately, I took their advice. In the words of Forrest Gump, "I… was… ru-un-ning!" And in case you hate to run, I'm not advocating running per se. I'm arguing that the contrarian church planter can't afford *not* to exercise.

Did you know that exercise is scientifically proven to be a stress reliever? When you have above-normal physical activity your body releases extra endorphins, which are the feel-good neurotransmitters of the brain. The term "runner's high" isn't just a cute phrase, it's a physiological fact. But it's not just referring to running; it refers to any activity that pumps up endorphins.

In addition to relieving stress, staying in shape gains the respect of those you are trying to reach. More than one third of Americans are now obese. As a nation we overeat, under-exercise, and under-sleep. By being in shape, you gain the respect of those you want to reach because discipline attracts followers.

For example, maybe the best way to grow is to practice spiritual disciplines. But how does it look when an overweight, out-of-shape preacher is asking people to be disciplined and read their Bibles? I think some of them are cynically saying, "*You* are telling *me* about discipline? Why don't you lay off the Big Gulps and then we'll talk?" The moment you get in shape you will have a more captive audience.

Also, getting in shape is good for you spiritually. Can I say something that sounds weird? You know what has happened with my running? The exercise has become a spiritual discipline. During my long runs is when I get my best prayer time, it's when I can clearly think through stressful situations at church, and it's when I'm able to process tough decisions.

When I think of balance, the thing I remember is the see-saw in preschool. One person sits at each end and you go back and forth, up and down, up and down. It was always crucial that you got someone of similar weight on the opposite end, because if not you'd be stuck in the air or stuck on the ground!

And that's the problem.

If you try to balance work and life, family and ministry, spiritual health and physical health, something will inevitably be out of balance. By realizing that balance is a myth, you will be set free to love your family, run after Jesus, have disciplines that fill you up, and plant a great church.

But nothing, nothing at all, is worse than getting your finances out of balance, which is what we'll talk about next.

Chapter 6

HONORING GOD FINANCIALLY

A new report indicated recently that doctors avoid discussing childhood obesity with parents. In the survey, 24 percent admitted feeling uncomfortable discussing a child's weight issues with the parents. This despite the fact that one third of all children suffer from obesity, which is now the leading cause of death in the United States.

I have two reactions to that story. One is sympathy. I wouldn't want to be the doctor who has to tell a parent: "YOU have to do something because you're putting your child on a collision course with an early death."

But of course, my other reaction is—outrage is maybe too strong of a word, but—outrage! These kids are on a collision course with death and you have a chance to stop it. You gotta speak up! That's what I feel like as I begin this chapter. Money is killing many church planters, yet we refuse to talk about it.

So how do we deal with money? My three-year-old daughter had a brilliant idea. She had gotten her first ever dollar bill. And she knew enough to understand the power that it held—that it could buy her a drink at Chick-Fil-A or gum at Target. So she wisely said, "Look, Daddy, now I have two" as she ripped it in half.

I'm guessing that's not a strategy Dave Ramsey teaches. But the reality is that every church plant reaches a point financially where you feel the need to magically multiply money. That stressful time of not enough money to cover the bills will happen. It may come during the pre-launch phase. It could be in year one or two, maybe even later than that. But the majority of church plants eventually have to make tough choices around money.

The question is how to avoid that problem. If there is a strategy you could employ now to avoid losing sleep about money, what would it be?

Yes, there was an earlier chapter in this book about money. That chapter focused on fundraising. This chapter will focus on how to handle money in a more general sense.

Billy Graham said, "If someone gets their perspective on money right, almost everything else will fall into place."

The reality is that ministry costs money. The other reality is that you have a limited amount of money. The solution, of course, is to tap into the greatest resource of all: God. We've all heard, or probably even quoted, the verse: "God owns the cattle on a thousand hills." So we know that he is fully capable of providing everything we need. The problem is that we try to manipulate him into giving us money.

***

It's always interesting to hear church leaders discuss why their churches are having money problems. You'll hear a whole range of excuses including:

- The economy is bad. (Translation: I have no idea why we are having money problems, but no one will argue with this.)
- Our congregation is selfish. (Translation: I am more spiritual than these people.)
- We reach really lost people. (Translation: We are so good at reaching the lost that we're victims and will be stuck poor forever.)
- We had too much faith. (Translation: we don't know how to budget.)

Obviously, I'm a little skeptical when people complain about money, but there are several responses church leaders have when they have money problems. Some people say nothing at all. Some leaders scold their people. Some throw a pity party for themselves that their people aren't more generous like that church down the street. Still others will teach and inspire their people to give more.

We all want to be the person who inspires their people to live with greater generosity. The problem is that conventional practice doesn't cut it.

> # The conventional practice is to have faith, and this is garbage.

I'm not saying that faith is garbage because Romans 1 says that's how we accept God's free gift of grace. But as a response to money problems, the simple answer of "have faith" is lazy, arrogant, and misguided. And if you're offended, that's not me saying this—it's God! Consider the following passages.

- Go to the ant, you sluggard; consider its ways and be wise! It has no commander, no overseer or ruler, yet it stores its provisions in summer and gathers its food at harvest. (Proverbs 6:6-8)
- Those who work their land will have abundant food, but those who chase fantasies have no sense. (Proverbs 12:11)
- All hard work brings a profit, but mere talk leads only to poverty. (Proverbs 14:23)

Over and over again the Bible condemns laziness but promises a reward for hard work. There's really nothing wrong with having faith, but as a money management strategy it's horrible and it's not in the Bible.

Here's how this "all-we've-gotta-do-is-have-faith" deal works out in reality. People express it as, *"If you give, you're good.*" Many Bible teachers espouse this way of thinking. And there are indeed numerous Scriptures that say if you give, God will provide. But I'm referring to the people who ignore every other verse about money and teach solely on giving. The extreme example of this is the televangelists who will sit on gold thrones with a gold piano talking about how they need more money (before they go home to their multi-million dollar mansions). They'll pontificate about how if you're in debt or you're sick then you still should put the needs of ministry above your health or your bills; then God will see that and bless you.

I like what one preacher said. He watched the televangelist promise that if you sent in 100 dollars then God would send you 1000. So the preacher called in and said, "How about *you* send *me* 100 dollars? Then God will give *you* the thousand dollars and we'll both be happy!"

So when a church planter stands in front of his church and says, "If you give, God will bless you," and leaves it at that, are we really any different from the televangelist? This leads to guilt and legalism among the people, and to frustration among the leadership. There has to be a better way.

The Better Way

I remember the first time I saw *The Wizard of Oz*. My parents were excited to show their oldest son this classic film. They got some popcorn ready, snuggled up under the blanket, and started the VHS tape. I was bored when I saw a black and white film start, then intrigued when it went to color, then captivated by the idea that I could visit a community where only little people live, then freaked out by flying monkeys.

But I distinctly remember in my six-year-old brain being very annoyed at the end of the film. Dorothy goes on a journey through Oz just so she can get back to Kansas. But in Oz, Glinda the good witch tells her, "You've always had the power to go back to Kansas." She then explains that if Dorothy clicks her heels together and says the magic phrase ("There's no place like home") she'll be whisked back to Kansas.

When I say this I thought, "What a ripoff! You should've told her that in munchkin land and saved me two hours!" (I didn't think Glinda was a very good witch after that.) The contrarian church planter knows that what was true for Dorothy in Oz is true for the church planter with money. But rather...

> # The contrarian's practice is not to honor God with a tithe, but with everything he gives you.

And this begins with your personal finances.

That's right. How your church is doing financially is directly related to how you manage the books at home. This is true simply because the church planter will set up the systems for how the church handles money. If you handle money poorly at home, you will handle money poorly at church. If you live on credit at home, you will live on credit at church.

And how you live at home is exaggerated when it comes to church finances, because you think, "This is spiritual. This is ministry. This is evangelism. So I have to spend money on this!" The Bible says, "You reap what you sow." With your lifestyle at home, you are sowing certain habits, and these are the habits with which you will run the church's finances.

So let me give you five keys to honoring God with ALL your money.

Way #1: Tithe

This is the number one priority of handling your money. This is, in fact, the one thing that Jesus commends the Pharisees for doing, being meticulous tithers, even off of their garden herbs. If you are not tithing, there is no reason your people will tithe. If you do, the people in your church will. If you don't, they won't. It really is that simple. Listen to what radio talk show host and financial expert Dave Ramsey said about tithing,

> "If Christians tithed, America would be a different place. There would be no more welfare in North America. In ninety days, there would be no existing church or hospital debts. In the next ninety days, the entire world could be evangelized. There would be prayer in schools, and the Ten Commandments on the walls because Christians would buy all the schools!"

When I preach on tithing I tell our people about the money back guarantee. The church I worked at in Virginia Beach, Virginia is called Forefront Church. And when they preach on giving they offer a money-back guarantee. They say, "If you give ten percent of your income to God for an entire year—not eight or five, but a full ten—and you do not feel God has blessed you, we will refund every penny you gave to Forefront." I'm going to offer that same guarantee: if you give ten percent to Mosaic for a year and feel that God has not blessed you because of it, Forefront Church in Virginia Beach will refund every penny!

Now I know a lot of Christians don't believe we should tithe. They'll accurately point out that it's not commanded after Jesus comes on the scene. And I agree that we shouldn't tithe. In fact, I believe that **we should do more than tithe.**

I've never understood the debate among Christians about whether or not we should tithe. We live in the richest country in the history of the world. Is there any reason we should be giving less than ten percent to our church and not being generous with other things as well? Do we really believe that church planting is the most effective evangelistic strategy on the face of the planet, or is that just convenient to say when we're fundraising? Do we really believe that there are a real heaven and a real hell and that everyone spends eternity in one or the other? Do we really believe that our little bit of giving can make an impact on someone's life, or is that just something we teach when the sermon is about giving?

The goal is to give as much as possible, not reach a

mere percentage and stop. The way one church planter does this practically is like this: he and his wife have a budget they live on. Years ago they started giving ten percent to their church, and a certain percentage on top of their church giving to give to other people and organizations. Each January they increase one of those by a quarter of a percent. Add that up over the course of the lifetime, and you're talking about some serious generosity!

The best example I've seen of a generous minister is a friend of mine named Dave. When Dave got married he and his wife combined barely made enough to equal one full salary. Still, he made a decision that for his entire marriage, the largest check he wrote each month would be to the church. That meant that Dave and his new bride had to find a cheap place to live. They scoured the Midwestern city where they lived until they found a widow who was renting out the basement of her house.

No matter what situation they found themselves in, whether it was a new job or having kids, Dave and his wife have consistently given the largest check each month to their church. Today Dave makes a good income and pastors one of the most generous churches I've ever heard of. Coincidence? I don't think so. Dave is a living example of what the Bible teaches: you will reap what you sow.

But it's not just about giving. There's more to handling money wisely than that. The contrarian church planter also recognizes that an important part of planting a church is to...

Way #2: Live debt free

I'll never forget the phone call. Our young church had

given financially to help another church get started in our state. This new church plant had formed a launch team, raised a lot of money, done multiple outreach events, bought equipment, and was set to meet in a school. The morning this new church was set to launch I texted the lead pastor to wish him luck. I knew the mixed emotions he was feeling of excitement and fear, so I encouraged him to enjoy the moment and soak it all in, and told him we'd pray for him in our service.

Within seconds my phone was ringing with a call from the planter. To answer I said, "Are you pumped?!" He responded, "Don't pray for us."

Confused, I asked why not and he responded, "We're not launching today."

Even more confused, I asked what was going on. Through tears, he went on to explain that the night before he had been fired by his management team after they learned of some financial improprieties on his part.

Apparently, he had been living in a cycle of debt for years. He had taken loans from people in his past church to pay back other debts. Finally, when more bills were due and he had no one else to ask, he used the church's checking account to pay someone back.

That's when the hidden cycle of debt came to light. And the worst part of it all? His wife didn't know any of this.

To make the story even more depressing, a couple hundred people showed up at the school that day. They were greeted by members of the management team, who told each car, "The church won't be launching today."

Then they watched those cars turn around and go home.

Debt can destroy you. That story is an extreme example, and the problem is that most of us have learned to manage our debt. We think it's not affecting us, but the Bible tells us otherwise. Proverbs 22:7 says,"The rich rule over the poor, and the borrower is slave to the lender."

Dave Ramsey gets people laughing about this when he wraps a chain around himself and shows how hard it is to move when you're a slave. But Dave (and anyone in debt) knows this is no laughing matter. Debt will supersede all of your priorities and distract you from the divine task God has called you to. Debt will keep you up at night worrying about how to pay the bills. Debt will make you take a second job, distracting you from pastoring. Debt will tempt you to steal money. Debt will want your church to grow so you can get a raise, not so people can find hope. Debt will prevent you from enjoying the vacation when you really need a break from the pressures of leading a church plant.

You've heard the stats, but I'll remind you anyway:

- 90 percent of marriages that end in divorce within the first seven years blame money. (It's like the man who called the police and reported that all of his wife's credit cards had been stolen. Then he added, "But don't look too hard for the thief. He's charging less than my wife ever did.")
- More young people filed bankruptcy than graduated from college last year. And colleges are losing more people to credit problems than to bad grades.
- *The Consumer Reports Money Book* states that the average consumer debt in America is $38,000,

while the average household income is $40,000.

- Average student loan debt at graduation: $19,400.
- The average consumer debt (which wouldn't count your house, but school loans, car loans, and credit card debt) for 28-year-olds: $66,000.
- Average credit card balance per home: $8,580, averaging 18.3% interest.
- More than 25 percent of the average family's income goes to debt retirement, not including their home mortgages.

> # You will be more effective as a church planter if you are debt free.

You will be more generous with your time, more present with your family, more able to relax on vacation, and more focused on reaching the lost.

The unfortunate truth is that church planters and church planting organizations have bought into the lie that "everyone else does it" so it's okay for church planters to be in debt too. But debt is killing pastors and destroying churches. It may not be as blatant as the church plant I described earlier, but it is like a river constantly pushing on a dam. Even if it doesn't crack, it's pressure the planter doesn't need. When it comes to debt the conventional practice is to act just like the surrounding culture when it comes to debt. But the contrarian church planter gets out of debt.

Your debt is making you a slave. You will not be the church planter God wants you to be as long as you are carrying debt. Break free from the chains of debt. Live counter-culturally. Your family, church, and community will get a better version of yourself as a result.

Way #3: Live by a budget

Unfortunately, this concept also is contrarian in today's day and age. Let's do an experiment to prove it. How much cash do you have on you right now? Do you know the total? What you'll find is that people who handle money well will know exactly how much they have on them: "$47 dollars!" The person who doesn't handle money well has no idea. The first person will tell you, "I have $28: one ten, three fives, and three ones, all folded in half in my right pocket." The second person says, "Uhhh, let's see....I've got a couple ones in this pocket. Oh, wow—there's a twenty in my coat pocket! I've also got some loose change—maybe a couple bucks there. And if I searched in my car I bet I could find a few more dollars if I have to go through a toll."

Church planters need to be different. We need to set an example of debt-free living. Our task is too important to just go with the flow of culture. One statistic I read said the average income in the United States is $43,000. If you only make the average income, and you work for 40 years you will handle 1.7 million dollars in your lifetime. If you're handling 1.7 million dollars you can't afford to "just go with the flow."

At the beginning of every month, my wife and I have a budget meeting. During the meeting, we decide where our money for the next month will go. We map it all out, knowing each month is different from the last. And we meet until we have agreed where every dollar will be spent.

Oh, and there's an important key to the budget: you have to follow the budget! If I see a new outfit, but our clothing budget is gone, I have to wait until next month. If I want to eat out but our eating out budget is gone, I eat cereal at home. You must discipline yourself to follow the budget.

Remember the parable of the talents. God has entrusted you with a certain amount of money and he is counting on you to manage it with wisdom. A budget is the best tool that will help you do this.

Way #4: Save

The last step to personal financial health is to save. When we say "save" we *don't* mean "hoard". Did you see the TV show *Hoarders*? It follows people around who can't get rid of anything. Often they have paths through their houses, with junk piled to the ceiling on either side. One lady had so much stuff that cats were breeding in her house—when they cleaned it out they found over 100 cats, most of them alive!

The worst case of hoarding I've read about was Heddy Green. She lived in a shack and ate cold oatmeal because she didn't want to use money cooking it. Everybody thought she was poverty-stricken because she only wore clothes from Goodwill, and she tried to find free medical care for her son so long he developed gangrene in his leg and had it amputated. When she died the only possessions they found in her house were four scraps of soap in a tin dish. But when Henrietta Holland Green died in 1916 she had an estate worth $95 million, including over $31 million in one bank account. That's the kind of woman you want for an aunt!

An important distinction as we talk about saving has to do with motive. The Bible clearly teaches us to save money for the future:

- Proverbs 21:20: "The wise store up choice food and olive oil, but fools gulp theirs down."
- Proverbs 6:6-8: "Go to the ant, you sluggard; consider its ways and be wise! It has no commander, no overseer or ruler, yet it stores its provisions in summer and gathers its food at harvest."
- Proverbs 11:26: "People curse the one who hoards grain, but they pray God's blessing on the one who is willing to sell."
- Ecclesiastes 5:13: "I have seen a grievous evil under the sun: wealth hoarded to the harm of its owners."

The motive for the hoarder is to selfishly save everything you can for himself. The motive for the godly saver is to not be a burden to others and to live a generous life.

So we need to save. Andy Stanley puts it like this when talking about debt and saving: "There are 2 types of people in the world: those who pay interest, and those who make interest."

Most of us are paying interest on debt, but the contrarian planter will turn that math on its head so that interest is working in our favor. Even if you can only save a little, over time it will build so that soon you have more than you dreamed was possible.

***

Some of you have been reading this, thinking, "Come on Carl, give me some tips for church planting, not personal finance. However...

> # What you sow in your personal finances, you will reap in your church's finances.

Church plants' finances tend to mirror the finances of the church planter. If the church planter doesn't live on a budget, neither will the church. If the church planter is generous with his personal finances, the church plant will give freely. If the church planter saves, the church plant plans for unforeseen expenses.

So the same things you do in your personal finances are what your church plant should do. This is why it is imperative that you have your personal finances in order. Speed of the leader, speed of the team! So let's revisit these from a church perspective.

Establish a baseline of generosity

Many church plants give a cut of their offerings to the organization that planted them or to their denomination. That's a good thing if that money is going to start future ministries. But whether it's forced or not, to your planting organization or not, find a way to establish a baseline of generosity. The way one church did this was to "tithe" on its offerings. They give 5 percent of their offerings to American church plants, 2.5 percent to global missions, and 2.5 percent as local benevolence. Whatever fits your culture in your setting, find a baseline of generosity to set, and don't waver from it.

Practice extravagant generosity

This is the point of Mary pouring perfume on Jesus, right? This is Barnabas selling land to support the church. This is the widow putting in her two mites. The church needs to blaze the trail of extravagant generosity. Remember the widow: extravagant doesn't mean big. It just means more than rationally makes sense. Mark Batterson talks about the first check his National Community Church wrote to missions. It was for only fifty dollars, but percentage-wise, that was the biggest check to missions he had ever written.

Another church plant recently challenged their two-year-old church to raise $25,000 above their normal giving. It was for a building campaign…but a different kind of building. They built a church in Ecuador. In addition, they challenged their church to adopt the kids in this village through Compassion International. So this small, new church is responsible for people in Central America having their own church building, as well as having schooling, clothes, and proper nutrition. That's extravagant!

And I love what Batterson adds: you can't outgive God! So practice extravagant generosity.

Get out of debt

Most church plants aren't in debt in the legal sense, because no one would be crazy enough to lend you money. The way this principle applies to church planting is to become self-supportive as quickly as possible. Many church planters will give reasons why this is difficult, why their people aren't giving. But this is why it is imperative for the lead planter to become debt free.

The average American gives away just under 3 percent of their income. Why isn't that higher? Some of it is probably selfishness, but I believe the biggest reason is debt. When 25 percent of your budget goes to debt (that doesn't even include your home mortgage), it's going to be hard for you to give away 10 percent and more to the church and other good causes. Few people say, "I don't want to be more generous." But plenty of people say, "I can't afford to be."

The biggest key to increasing giving at your church is to teach your people to get out of debt. The simple truth is that a lot of them want to give, but they can't under their current debt load. Teach them how to be debt free, practice generosity, and you will see them give.

Live on a budget

I'm a believer that churches need detailed budgets in order to manage God's money wisely. But there are two errors that churches make with budgets. The first is not being specific enough. Some churches don't even have a budget at all! I asked one planter what his budget was and he scoffed, "Budget? We just spend what it takes to get the job done!" That would be funny if the Bible didn't talk over and over about us being good stewards of what God gives us.

The other extreme is people following a budget too rigidly. It's true that if you don't live by a budget it's useless. Living out what the budget says is the tough part. But be willing to change the budget. Creating a personal budget is easier because you've been spending in those areas for years. If this is your first church plant, it's difficult to figure out where all the money will go. Maybe you need to do with your church what Dave Ramsey teaches for individuals: make a brand new budget each month. But however often you do it, live on a budget.

Save

This is super contrarian. Carl, how can our church save when we're living week to week on our tiny offerings? Besides, what should we save *for*? The truth is I don't know. And that's the point. Savings are for what you can't see coming. Let me say that I believe one of Satan's best tactics to impede church plants is to distract the planter with financial worry, and one of the best ways to accomplish that is by the church not having a contingency fund in case it's needed.

In the last ten years, I have seen three different church

plants create a savings account, and from day one they put a percentage of their offerings in there. One is now a huge megachurch. One was able to buy land in an expensive area in California with their savings. The third is just a couple years old at this point and is self-supportive, even though they were a parachute plant with multiple staff.

When you save, the stress of money leaves your church plant. Our church decided to follow the example of others, and from the outset, we have saved 10 percent of all our offerings. Is it for an outreach event? No. Is it for a building? No. What's it for? The truth is we don't know, and again, that's the point. But we know that when God presents a big opportunity we'll be ready.

And the byproduct is stress-free planting, at least as far as money is concerned. We've never not made payroll. We've never called our landlord to ask for an extension on rent. We've never not been able to replace an important piece of equipment that broke.

Now I know what you're thinking: "We can't afford to save!" Neither could those three churches when they first launched. But they chose a percentage of their budget to designate as savings, and they found a way to make things work. And it's not that you can't afford to save; **you can't afford not to save!**

Saving creates a buffer between you and financial emergency. It gives peace of mind so you can focus on important things like fixing marriages and accountability for the addict instead of distracting things like how are we going to make payroll. Yes, we trust God to provide. But he's providing *now* for your future, so save and get ready.

***

I want to share one last personal story on why I think personal finances matter so much. When I was in high school. my church did a massive capital campaign so they could construct a new building. They were asking everyone in the church to make a three-year commitment, and I got caught up in the emotion of it and didn't really plan well and committed to giving about 800 dollars over the three years to the campaign. The problem was I didn't have any money! So I was able to give maybe $100 of it and then I got behind and just stopped. Forgot about it. They got the building—I went on to college. It all worked out.

But in May of 2002, I was getting ready to graduate from college. I had a yearlong internship set up in Virginia, and I was ready to go work in a church for the first time. One morning in my daily Bible reading I was reading in Jonah and from the belly of the fish Jonah said to God, "I will fulfill my vow to you."

And that hit me like a ton of bricks. It was one of those "oh crap" encounters with God. I got chills in my spine because I knew I had a choice to listen to God's Spirit or to ignore him and do my own thing. See, I had about 800 dollars in my bank account at the time. I wasn't going to hardly get paid during my internship, so that was going to be my financial cushion. But I could not get that stinking verse out of my head....and believe me, I tried!

So I wrote a check for the balance and included a note that said, "I know you're already in the building so you probably don't need this. But I believe out of obedience to God that I need to give this. I'm really sorry it took me eight years to fulfill a three-year commitment, but I couldn't think of starting a career working in the church with this hanging over my conscience."

What it came down to was—was I going to trust God? Was I going to live out what the Bible teaches about finances and begin my ministry debt free? It's embarrassing that it took me eight years to show my trust in God with a mere few hundred dollars. I pray it doesn't take you as long.

But do you trust him? I know you trust him with your eternity. I know you trust him to answer prayer. But do you trust him when he tells us in the Bible how to take care of money?

They say the way you can know what's important to someone is to look at their calendar and their bank statements. Listen: when you look at your online bank statement—whether you are a high school student with a part-time job, a single person with a starter position, or a parent with special needs—do you trust him?

If so, let's talk about some more numbers that matter to God, and therefore must matter to us.

Chapter 7

NUMBERS MATTER

The most frightening experience of my life was the moment I realized I lost my daughter.

Let me explain. The way our townhouse is set up is the first floor is like the basement. The second floor has the kitchen and family room. So a couple years ago the four of us were all on the second floor like normal when my wife Lindsay asks, "Where's Reagan?" Reagan was two at the time and knew she wasn't allowed downstairs. But she had snuck downstairs, so I go down there and look around and I holler up to Lindsay, "She's not down here!" Then I look at our front door, and it's cracked open. This sends chills down my spine because I didn't even know Reagan could unlock a door, let alone a deadbolt lock. I holler up: "She went outside!"

I walk outside, fully expecting to see my cute little toddler playing in our small patch of grass. But instantly my heart sinks because she's not there. So I run inside and yell, "I don't see her!" I run outside and start looking around…no Reagan. I run behind our house to look on the playground.…no Reagan. By this time Lindsay has started running in the opposite direction while holding our four-month-old boy, Quint. We have no idea how long Reagan's been gone. *Where is she? Has someone taken her? Did she find a toy in someone's backyard?* I hop on my bike and start riding around, hoping that she found some cool toy in someone's backyard.…no Reagan. I ride back to our house, not sure what else to do. Lindsay is not yelling, but she's screaming Reagan's name in a guttural way that only a mother can. At this point, Lindsay runs inside, sprints up the stairs to grab her phone to call 911. But right when she reaches her phone, she glances out the window and sees a brown ponytail walking down the street, about sixty houses away.

Lindsay jumps outside, sprints to Reagan, still screaming her name. By this point, Reagan's met one of our neighbors out walking her dog and having the time of her life petting this dog. So Lindsay runs up screaming her name in fear and joy, tears streaming down her face. And Reagan turns around kind of freaked out because she was oblivious, just enjoying her canine experience! Lindsay hugged her and wouldn't let go.

That was a traumatic experience on my wife and me. Lots of horrible thoughts raced through our minds during those minutes that seemed like hours when Reagan was gone. I can't even type the things I was thinking because they are so horrific and scary.

But you know one thing that never went through our minds: "At least we've still got Quint!" We didn't rationalize. *Reagan's disobedient a lot. We've still got one kid. A lot of our friends can't even have children, so one is still good. One kid would actually be easier anyway. We're okay without her.* We never thought those things! Our kid was gone, and we needed her home!

The Bible is clear that Jesus died to bring his lost children home. Jesus himself said that he came to seek and to save the lost (Luke 19:10). It doesn't get much clearer than that.

In our situation with Reagan, here's the simplified version of our problem: our family had four people in it. But we only knew where three were. So our family of three needed to become a family of four again.

In light of the mission, Jesus declared for his life and for the church, here is the contrarian wisdom of this chapter: Numbers matter in church planting. This is not something many church planters embrace. In fact, the conventional practice is to use stories to gauge health.

There are several reasons we embrace story instead of numbers. For one thing, stories are more interesting. If you are at a church planting conference and someone hands out an Excel spreadsheet, your eyes would glaze over and you'd struggle to stay awake. But if the speaker tells a dramatic story of a raging alcoholic who came to Christ when they were on the verge of suicide and that person now leads a recovery ministry to homeless veterans, you're on the edge of your seat. Stories are more interesting than numbers.

Stories are also emotional. Numbers don't make you

laugh and cry; stories do. This means that stories motivate people to fund your church plant, stories get people on board with your vision, stories inspire us to change.

Additionally, stories are easier. If I'm writing a sermon on addiction, it's much easier to tell the story of the man freed from addiction than to come up with data on what helps people like him. The majority of the time, telling a story is a simpler way to communicate.

But there's a problem with stories: they don't tell the whole truth. See, here's what happens with stories. You can use a story to prove anything you want. In the first church I worked, one week we were in a meeting debating using a particular type of song in our worship service. I had recently had someone complain to me that their non-Christian friend wouldn't attend our church because of that style of music. Since our goal was to reach non-Christians with the Gospel, this was a pretty compelling argument. But when I brought it up, someone else in the meeting interrupted with a story of their own, explaining that type of music is the very reason another person had stayed at our church, where he was eventually baptized and now led a ministry.

So who was right? Which opinion of the best way to reach people prevailed? Typically it's the person who is the best storyteller. And that's not a great way to make important decisions.

You can find a story to back up any opinion. Taking the above scenario to another level, I could have found *someone* in our church to disagree with just about any single thing we did. I could have told that story to argue a certain opinion I had. But that raises questions: for how many people is that their story? If it's one person's story, does that mean it's everyone's story? Should I base big decisions off that story, or is it an anomaly?

Stories inspire us. What's wrong with this? It's good to inspire people, right? Well, yes....*if*—and that's a big *if*—you're leading them in the right direction. If you have gotten off course of where God wants to lead your church, even just a little, inspiring people down that direction is taking them away from God's will. Then you're getting people emotionally attached to something that may not be where God wants them in the first place.

Don't get the wrong impression here: the contrarian church planter uses the power of stories to inspire, cast vision, and raise money. But because they are so powerful, he understands they must be based on something more than a passing emotion.

Let me illustrate it this way. A man in our church recently went to the doctor for a checkup on his leukemia that's been in remission for a couple years. The doctor asked how he felt, and he told stories of feeling healthy and doing fun things and enjoying life with his family. Unfortunately, when they did the blood work, the numbers told a different story. His white blood count should have been under 10,000. His was over 300,000. At that moment, it didn't matter how good he felt or what story he could tell about leading a normal lifestyle. The only thing that mattered was the data.

In the world of church planting, sometimes we're like the man going to the doctor who wants to tell a story when instead we need to look at the data. Here's what the contrarian understands: we must use numbers to tell the whole truth.

I know most of you just cringed at that because I wrote it, and I cringed at it, too! We have a legitimate problem with numbers. Our unease stems from the fact that we have seen people use the wrong numbers and use numbers in wrong ways.

We have seen people measure the wrong things, rendering the numbers ineffective. Since 2007, the Massachusetts Institute of Technology has hosted an event each year called the Sloan Sports Analytics Conference. It's essentially a few days of geeks arguing about what stats are important in sports. At an interview with ESPN, several of its leaders agreed that in twenty years no one in the NBA will care about points per game or rebounds per game, because those stats have zero correlation with wins. They just show individual ability and are cool to boast about.

We've seen the exact same thing in church, haven't we? The typical ABCs of measurement—attendance, buildings, and cash—don't necessarily show if your church is "winning". They show some of your church's ability and they can be fun to brag about. But they are inadequate much of the time.

Often churches don't measure enough, meaning the data is inadequate. One church plant hosts an annual "Trunk or Treat" outreach event every Halloween. Their attendance kept increasing year after year, which was great. But after a couple years, they realized that they didn't know if it was reaching non-Christians (the target audience) or simply drawing a bunch of Christians from other churches.

They had to find a new way to measure so they knew if the event was effective. If we don't measure enough of the right things, we will have inadequate data that doesn't tell us what we need to know.

Numbers lead to insecurity. This is where we really get in trouble, because we have seen numbers increase but character decrease. And the Bible backs this up. In 2 Samuel 24, David takes a census to determine how big his army is. His commander Joab recognizes the pride that motivates David and tries to stop him, but David won't have it and the census proceeds. After the census is complete, David realizes his guilt for taking pride in how big his army is and he repents. Unfortunately, it's too late. God sends a plague on Israel, and the Bible reports that 70,000 of God's people died as a result of David's pride and insecurity.

Remember there is nothing wrong with a census in and of itself. God himself had commanded a census in Numbers chapter one. The difference is motive.

Let's say that when you get home from work today your wife is wearing the best-looking dress she owns. She is wearing brand new, stylish shoes. She went out and got her hair and nails done. She's put on just the right amount of makeup. And when you see her, your eyes get big and you say, "Girl, you look gooood!"

Now let's say that in response she smiles and says, "Thanks. I'm going dancing with the girls tonight and I want to impress all the guys there."

Umm, excuse me? That's horrible! That is entirely different than if she said, "Hurry up and change. I got a babysitter and reservations—we're going on a hot date tonight." Boo-ya! It's the motive that determines the validity of the action.

***

Have you noticed the love/hate relationship that pastors have with numbers?

- If our attendance was low last week then measuring attendance is superficial, so who cares anyway?
- If our offering is high people are behind the vision.
- If the offering is low then we're doing a good job of reaching lost people.
- On Easter suddenly attendance is very spiritual again.
- If our number of groups is static, we say that we're building deep community, so the number doesn't really matter.
- If our groups are multiplying, then the numbers are important again.

In fact, a lot of pastors suffer from a disease I call Attendicitis:

The causes of attendicitis are a low number of butts in seats, a lack of dollars in the bank, and exposure to large ministries. Attendicitis is caught at large church conferences and through reading books from well-known pastors. Symptoms include depression, feelings of worthlessness, emotional absence from wife and kids, a dazed look, and utter exhaustion. Curiously, attendicitis flare-ups are more common on Sunday afternoons and Monday mornings than any other time of the week.

The reaction of some pastors to attendicitis is to not measure anything. You'd rather be an ostrich with your head stuck in the sand than know the sad reality of your situation. Or you hide behind a mask of ultra-spirituality and say numbers don't matter.

But remember how many numbers are in the Bible.

- God takes a census in Numbers 1.
- From Christ's ministry, how do we know Jesus fed 5,000 and then 4,000? Because someone counted.
- God went to extreme detail for the measurements of his Temple because its precision was important.
- We know that 3,000 gave their lives to Jesus the day the church was born in Acts 2.
- My favorite number in the Bible is 153. That's the number of fish Peter and the other disciples caught in John 21 after Jesus rose from the dead. Even though the biggest part of the story is that Jesus rose from the grave, someone went to the trouble of counting all the slimy, stinky fish just to show how amazing Jesus was.

The Bible measures things because numbers matter to God. And numbers matter to God because people matter to God. Here's why I love numbers when it comes to church planting:

> # Numbers don't have feelings. They are impartial.

Often when we make ministry decisions, the consequences affect people emotionally. Do we stop a particular ministry? Do we start a new one? What group do we cater to? What group can we not reach at this time? Those are very emotional decisions! People can get feelings hurt, mad, or bitter.

If I am making those decisions based just on what I feel is correct, I had better be very discerning and have a lot of leadership capital to spend with people. If our church makes decisions based on data, then it's not about me and my opinion, but simply what's best for our church.

Let's use a very simple example. Say you have two services at church at 8 A.M. and 10 A.M. You notice that you are running out of seats at 10, but have plenty of seats at 8. So you shift the service times to 9 am and 11 am. You count the number of empty seats, and immediately you can tell the services have evened out. So there is now room for non-Christians at both services, which there wasn't before. But then someone complains and says, "Because of my work schedule, I could only come at 8. Now I can't come to service anymore!" Because you rely on numbers, you know that this is the best decision to reach the most people, regardless of anyone's feeling or one particular story. It doesn't make it easier for that one person, but because numbers don't have feelings you know it's the best decision to reach more people.

Numbers tell a story.

Often we think the opposite is true, so we focus on

anecdotes rather than numbers. Specifically, pastors are famous for doing this regarding church health.

A megachurch pastor spoke at an event recently, detailing his church's transition in style. For a couple decades, his church had an attractional style of ministry. And it worked: thousands came, hundreds went on mission trips, hundreds were baptized. But a couple decades in he began to notice that couples who had been coming for years were getting divorced. Friends were paying for their teenage daughters to have abortions. So-called Christians weren't giving anything.

So this pastor became convinced it wasn't working and has completely revamped his church's model of ministry. And while he spoke in glowing terms about new relationships, he never shared any numbers.

His questions should have been: Are fewer people getting divorced in this model? Is generosity increasing? Are abortions down?

Without knowing the data, he's just going on his gut, and that's a bad thing to go on! Numbers tell a story. It could be a good story or a bad story. But it's an accurate story.

Numbers show improvement.

If you want your church to improve in areas of mission, giving, service, measure it! You can't tell those things by just doing an anecdotal survey. You need data. So if you want to emphasize missions more, is the percentage of Sunday attendance that goes on a short-term trip greater than last year? If your church needs to grow in love of the Bible, are more people reading daily than were six months ago? If you are putting on an outreach event for non-Christians, how many of the attendees are already attending another Bible-believing church?

Numbers are one indicator of health.

What if you went to the doctor when you had a serious illness. But instead of measuring your white blood cell count to see if you were healthy the doctor said, "We're not about numbers here...just tell me how you *feel* and we'll base our diagnosis on that." You'd find a new doctor! You'd want to know if you were getting sicker or healthier.

A friend of mine didn't measure his attendance for the first three years of his church plant. It was a philosophical decision, where he didn't want to base success on numbers. But in year three he was getting depressed about not growing and about low offerings. I asked him if he *knew* they weren't growing, but he couldn't answer for sure. Without taking attendance he didn't know if they were reaching more people with the message of the Gospel. Now he takes attendance each week and he *knows* if he should react to the numbers or not.

Numbers give God glory.

Because our church measures Sunday attendance consistently and accurately, we can praise God for the increase in attendance we've had each year. If we didn't count how many were there, we would have a vague idea that God was doing something special in our church, but we wouldn't be able to accurately thank him for what's going on.

> # It may be that if you don't count things in your ministry, and count well, that shows a lack of faith in God.

You might mask it behind a fake humility that says, "It's not about the number," but tell that to a Heavenly Father who has lost his child, because to him it is about a number.

We made a YouTube video at Mosaic a while ago that showcased the first five hundred people to get baptized at our church. We started with where they were before they met Jesus. Here are some quotations from the people we filmed.

"My dad died of heart disease when I was six. My mom overdosed when I was ten."

"I was a workaholic people pleaser, desperate for acceptance."

"I was an atheist for forty years."

"I grew up in an abusive home and abandoned by my mom.

"I felt judged and hated by Christians because I'm gay."

"Dead-end relationships left me feeling used, tired, and worthless."

Then we let those same people tell how Jesus began to

change their lives, all the way to number five hundred. The point the video makes is that we measure numbers because each number represents a story of life change, of someone finding true life in Jesus Christ. This is why numbers matter.

You are the Oakland A's, not the New York Yankees.

Did you see *Moneyball*? If not, you should! It was nominated for six Academy Awards and details the story of how the 2002 Oakland A's went to the playoffs with one of the smallest payrolls in baseball.

In 2002, the A's had a payroll of $41 million, while the Yankees' payroll exceeded $125 million. Even though the players on the field were playing the same game, the front office realized they couldn't function the same way that the Yankees did. Simply put: they couldn't afford to pay the top players. They needed a new metric, so they found new ways to build a team. They didn't use old measurements like batting average and RBI. Instead, they used on-base percentage, walks, and even how many pitches they took, a process called sabermetrics.

The book version of this story lists three mistakes that teams make in judging talent.

1. The tendency of everyone who actually played the game to generalize wildly from his own experience.
2. The tendency to be overly influenced by a player's most recent performance.
3. A bias towards what people saw with their own eyes.

So they came up with a new system. And it worked. The 2002 A's set an American League record with 20 wins in a row, a record that lasted for fifteen years. They made the playoffs, falling to the Minnesota Twins three games to two. The Boston Red Sox employed sabermetrics the following year and won the World Series for the first time in over eighty years.

As a church planter, you are the Oakland A's, for two reasons: 1) You will never have enough money, and 2) Your job is to win with what you have, not what you wish you could afford.

Andy Stanley has a great book called *The Seven Practices of Effective Ministry*, in which he states that you must define "the win". But the contrarian church planter must go farther than that and figure out how to *measure* the win.

Our church's vision is to be *a church for people who don't go to church*. So our number one goal is evangelism. How do we measure that? We could measure attendance, but how do we know if we're reaching non-Christians? We could measure baptisms, but as we grow we should naturally have more baptisms. So **the primary metric we use is baptisms as a percentage of attendance**. Assuming our attendance increases each year (and yes, that is a big assumption), the way we measure our evangelistic effectiveness is what percentage of those people are getting baptized.

Now that assumes our attendance is increasing, so we look at another metric to increase that. We've realized that our attendance increases when our percentage of second-timer guests to first-time guests goes up. We can't control attendance each and every week. But I can impact that smaller number of how many first-time visitors return for a second visit. If we are reaching out to them proactively without overstepping our bounds, they are more likely to come back a second time, and our attendance goes up when the percentage of people who do that increases.

Again, if we didn't keep track of numbers we wouldn't know this. We'd just guess that maybe we needed to reach out to first-timers more. But we wouldn't have empirical evidence to know if it was worth our time or not. Now, when I'm going through the boring task of writing handwritten note after handwritten note to our first-time guests, I have data that shows me it's a worthwhile task.

Now, remember the chapter on being who you want to be. I'm not saying these are necessarily the things you should measure. Don't copy us necessarily. For you there may be all sorts of things to measure:

- Percentage of Sunday attendance that goes on a foreign mission trip
- Number of hours your small groups are serving their communities
- Percentage of people who tithe
- Percent of people who pray daily

But whatever your "win" is, figure out how to measure that. Then if you want to do a drastic change in your ministry, you have data to show why you should do it, and whether or not the new way is more effective. By the way, I know a lot of you aren't numbers geeks. Most church planters aren't. But your ministry will be more effective if you track this stuff, so if this isn't your passion, find someone you trust on your team who can watch this stuff. And make sure it is someone you trust so that when they tell you the model you're in love with no longer works, you will listen!

What do you measure for discipleship? This is the question, right? I can measure the characteristics of the corporate church more easily than I can measure someone's soul. This is difficult. Fortunately, Greg Hawkins has helped us.

Greg is the person at Willow Creek Community Church who spearheaded their study called *Reveal*. This study sought to answer the question: does what we do create disciples? They interviewed tens of thousands of people at hundreds of churches across the country. The study resulted in a series of books, the best and most detailed of which is *Move*. They discovered catalysts that help people move from one spiritual level to the next. They realized that among people in church, there are four different divisions of spirituality, from "exploring Christ" to "Christ-centered".

But here's the most interesting part of what they found: "Reflection on Scripture is, by far, the most influential personal spiritual practice for every segment and across all [levels of spirituality]. ...Of all the personal spiritual practices, we find that reflection on scripture is much more influential than any other practice by a significant margin. In fact ... it's twice as catalytic as any other factor." (p. 117)

Now there are lots of possible applications of that. But the bottom line is they found what makes people grow, and they're measuring the win based on that.

Before I wrap up this chapter, let me remind you why this is so important:

- There are 195 million unchurched people in the United States.
- Each year 7,000 churches in the U.S. close their doors, but only 4,000 new ones are planted.

But the most important number is one. One person is all it took for Jesus to die on the cross. One person saved is all it takes to make a successful church plant. One person rescued from the fires of hell is our job at hand. Yes, we would love to reach all 200 million non-Christians in the United States, but we have to focus on the one that we can impact, the one in front of us, the one we will introduce to Jesus.

Eleven-year-old Shawn Hornbeck went for a bike ride on October 6, 2002. But he never came home. He was kidnapped, and police were unable to find Shawn or the kidnapper. The days turned into weeks, which turned into months and then years. Still no Shawn. A parent's little boy, gone. They didn't know who took him, why they had done it, what was happening to him, or if he was even still alive. Every day a living nightmare for a parent.

But on January 12, 2007, police were investigating another kidnapping and entered the home of a local pizzeria manager. They were astonished to discover a 16-year-old boy...named Shawn Hornbeck. After 1,558 days apart, Shawn and his dad were reunited.

I'll never forget watching the press conference with Shawn's dad. Here are some excerpts of what he shared that day:

"Obviously, this is probably the best day of our lives. It's hard to even come up with words that can express the feeling that we've been going through since 4:00 yesterday afternoon when we received the phone call. We were on our way home from work yesterday driving home in the miserable rain and nasty stuff when we got the call that they believed that Shawn had been found and that he was okay. I think it's probably the phone call that I'll remember most for the rest of my life..."

One of the primary reasons we're here today and doing this today is for those other parents out there that do have missing children... To give some of that fuel to some of the other parents that are in this situation, to let them know that miracles do happen, good things can happen. They don't always end bad.

...You can't lose hope. There's been many times where we investigated leads that took us down a road that we didn't want to go, but that's a road we had to go down just because you have to find out. That doesn't mean we lost hope. I've been asked a lot of times, what do you think happened? And you know, I've always said, you know, I don't really have an opinion as to what happened. I know what the predominant stories are. I know what I've heard over and over and over.

And, you know, 99 percent of those were very unpleasant stories, and it's hard not to give up hope when you just hear this over and over and over. But hope's the only thing that you have. Hope keeps you going. Hope keeps you alive. Hope gets you up in the morning. You know, I've always thought that, once you lose hope, it's over. You're done. And I promised not to lose hope, not to stop looking, and I've said all along, we will not stop until we find Shawn. Well, by God, here we are.

We have a Father in heaven whose children have been kidnapped by the enemy. You better believe he knows the exact number of those children. And he's not sitting in Heaven saying, "At least I've still got Carl." He has called you to bring his lost children home. Numbers matter because lost people matter. Let's bring them home.

Now let's turn to some advice that—if you follow it—will help you reach zero lost people.

Chapter 8

HOW TO HAVE AN AFFAIR

Following the trend of videos, two guys named Tripp and Tyler produced a "Stuff Nobody Says" video. Included among the quotes were the following.

- My Bazooka gum still has flavor.
- Baggy t-shirts look awesome on you.
- I miss faxing.
- Mmmmm, Captain D's.
- I completely understand my taxes.
- I'm hoping he asks me to help him move.
- I'm so glad I ate six chalupas.
- I just got the best deal on printer ink.
- I miss dial-up.
- Touch the screen.
- We should move to Oakland.
- I've never seen this IKEA furniture in anyone's

apartment.
- Could you please keep smacking your gum?
- I could really go for a Filet o' Fish right now.

Right now I want to teach you something that nobody says. It's a little different. I encourage you to stick with me before you judge me. I'm going to teach you how to have an affair! There are about six steps to having an affair, so I'll go through these one at a time.

I haven't had an affair. Neither has my wife. So I'm not sharing these out of personal knowledge, but these are based largely on the work of Pastor Ed Young and psychologist Dr. Jay Lindsey. I think they'll be very helpful for you if your marriage is stale or if you need some more excitement in your life.

So let's get into it. Here's how to have an affair. I'm going to skip the first step and come back to that because I think it only makes sense in light of these other ones.

Step #2 is to CULTIVATE a relationship with someone else.

This takes some time. First, you just need to be around some other people to see what happens. Rick Warren, megachurch pastor and author of the New York Times bestseller *The Purpose Driven Life*, said about sexual temptation, "I'm naturally inclined to have sex with every beautiful woman I see." So since that's how we're made, a step to having an affair is cultivating a relationship. It can start in public, maybe being in a group at your kids' school or at church. Then it can be just you two in private, so maybe you find ways to work late together. Or she's the only one who can give you a ride. You can just happen to go to the gym at the same times.

A great way to cultivate a relationship is with communication and flirtation. So you send her an email saying, "I really appreciate the way you listen when I talk about the problems I'm having with my wife." Get a lot of inside jokes together and things that really aren't that funny but he laughs at them anyway.

A great way to cultivate a relationship is how you dress. When you're going to be around her at work pick out your best outfits. If you're going to see him at the gym wear something tight and revealing. Even just to take care of yourself is a great way to cultivate a relationship: Do your hair up; if you can work out or get in shape, get thin.

Cultivate a relationship. People don't act like in the movies where they just meet for the first time and have sex two minutes later. You've got to cultivate this thing.

Step #3 is to COMPARE

Compare this person to your spouse. This is great in leading to an affair. Compare everything he/she does. Compare his reactions. Compare the way she dresses. Compare his breath. Compare her hairstyle.

Another great way to compare is to look at pornography. You can spend minutes or spend hours each day in your mind comparing bodies. And you don't even have to look at pornography You can find lots of great stuff out there that's not technically "porn" to compare. Find ways to fantasize about this.

Think thoughts like, What would it be like to spend

more time with them alone? What would it be like to hold them? That's not that bad, it's kind of innocent, right?. What would it be like just to go out to lunch with them alone? It's just fantasy! What would it be like to have sexual relations with them?

Let me add something for the single planters here: a great way to set yourself up for an affair is to have sex before you're married. If you have sex before you're married you'll do a lot better at this because you're training both your mind and your body that sex isn't saved just for marriage.

Step #4 is AFFECTION

We're not even talking about anything serious. Everyone needs a hug sometimes. You just need to express support. Maybe they need a back rub to loosen them up. All along these steps keep thinking: *I can cut it off at any time. This isn't hurting anyone. I'm okay.*

But then we come to the next step. Things get passionate. There's no denying there's some chemistry here. When you are together, sparks fly; a connection is taking place. Maybe you kiss, maybe it's just a longer embrace. And it makes you feel alive!

Step #5 is SEX

The urge, the connection is so strong that you live out your fantasy. There is still one more step.

Step #6 is ACCEPTANCE

This is where it's not just a heat of the moment thing—

this is where you say you were made for each other. This is right. I married the wrong person. God will forgive me. God wants me to be happy.

I skipped the first step because I think they only make sense in light of these other ones.

Here is **Step #1: BE PROUD!**

To set yourself up for an affair, think that you're above this. Put your marriage on cruise control! To see this you don't have to look any further than David. David, the Bible says, was a man after God's own heart, yet he committed adultery that the entire nation knew about. So be proud! Say, "this will never happen to me." Act like this would never happen to you—throw caution to the wind. And you can start walking down these steps. And eventually, you'll get to Step #6 where you'll say, "Well, God wants me to be happy!"

Okay, let's pause our little mental exercise there. I don't want you to have an affair! Unfortunately, this story is all too common. And not just among the general population; it's all too common among church planters. When one of my friends went through the church plant assessment process he was told, "Your personality is the most likely to have an affair." That's not exactly an encouraging conversation!

A Google search of "pastor affair resign" yields 1.5 million results as of this writing. 77 percent of pastors do not feel they have a good marriage. 30 percent either have an ongoing affair or a one-time sexual encounter with a parishioner. 40 percent of pastors polled said they have had an extra-marital affair since beginning their ministry.

The seventh commandment plainly states: Do not commit adultery. My fear is that this command is so shunned, looked down on, and outdated in our society that many of us cross some of these steps towards having an affair because no one cares if we do!

But this brings pain. About twice a year, just to scare myself into integrity, I actually Google "pastor affair resign." There is never a lack of recent results. I want to read you a letter that was written to Ed Young, a former pastor:

Dear Ed,

Our marriage was not perfect but it was ours and it was all we knew. He was my best friend and I trusted him totally. There were signs, I didn't ignore them, but I became suspicious and very observant. I finally got up the nerve to ask him point blank, face to face, "Are you and your co-worker having an affair?" My husband, and best friend of many years, looked me right in the eyes and lied.

There were times when I knew he was talking with her on the phone. Many times I would put my hand on the phone receiver by my bed and consider picking it up and listening; then I'd know for certain. No more speculating, but I couldn't do it because if it were true, it would hurt too much and what would I do?

Finally, my suspicions were replaced with fact. My thoughts and actions spun out of control. I became obsessed with the lies, the details of the affair, and the events that led to it. I kept trying to put all the puzzle pieces together. I was taken over by obsessions. Images of my husband and his lover would flash through my mind day and night. I constantly woke to dreams of him and her in bed together. It would play over and over and over. I stopped feeling positive about myself and about life. It was all negative, jealous, enraged, diminished, bitter, frightened, lonely, ugly, mistrustful, exposed.

His deception blinded me from how I saw myself. I started doubting and questioning everything about myself. I thought it must be me. I must have caused this affair to happen. I must change myself. I felt the fate of our marriage was in my hands.

Nobody's story ever goes like this: "My childhood was going okay until my dad cheated on my mom and had an affair. Then everything changed for the better!" Nobody ever says, "The highlight of my life was divorce proceedings and sitting down and explaining to my kids why I wouldn't see them at night anymore."

So God tells us "Do not commit adultery." Jesus even takes it a step further, pointing out that it's not about the letter of the law; it's the intent. He says not even to lust. The truth is many of us—maybe all of us?—have crossed one of these lines. So I want to spend just a minute addressing: How do we respond when we *have* crossed one of these lines?

The tricky thing about this is that sometimes it seems like having the affair or getting the divorce or leaving the kids would be better. Your marriage is that bad. And you're thinking, "Carl, compared to my situation an affair that adds excitement would be way better. I may hurt people, but at least I'd finally have some fun." Too many people have looked at Jesus' command and thought, "That's all that's required."

> # God's dream for your marriage isn't faithfulness. It's fulfillment.

He doesn't just want you to be faithful; that's the path to a fulfilling marriage.

So let's back this up. I want to give you some steps to a healthy, fulfilling marriage. And what you'll see very quickly is that these steps are the same to having a great marriage. Again, we'll start part way down.

Step #2: CULTIVATE a relationship with your spouse

Cultivate it behind their back. Here's what I mean: only talk about your spouse in a positive light. My wife is great at this. My wife has issues with me sometimes, but you know who will never know about it? You. And it's not that we hide it, because once we've worked through it we'll talk openly about it. But if she has an issue you know who she talks to? Me!

Let me write to the women for a moment. Some of you are anxious for your husband to cultivate a relationship with you, and you don't realize you've cut it off because you're talking about his issues on Facebook or on the phone or over coffee with the girls. If it gets back to him that you've been talking about him negatively he's done. Ephesians 5:33 says, "Each one of you also must love his wife as he loves himself, and the wife must respect her husband." A man's ego is huge and you can argue about it and say he shouldn't react that way, but he's done.

Men, I'm going to pick on you now. A lot of you make fun of your wives. And not only do you do it behind her back, you'll do it to her face. And you'll excuse it by saying it's a true story, that you're just sharing what really happened, but your body language and your making-fun-of-it tone betrays that you're really putting her down. Men, the rest of us aren't impressed. In fact, when you do that, we feel sorry for you because you have to put down your wife—a woman, God's daughter—to make yourself feel good. We see how pathetic that is and feel sorry for you. Because you know who does that? Boys! Men don't do that. 1 Peter 3:7 says, "Husbands, in the same way be considerate as you live with your wives, and treat them with respect as the weaker partner and as heirs with you of the gracious gift of life, so that nothing will hinder your prayers." Men are secure because Christ loves them, so men love their wives as Christ loved the church.

You know who makes fun of women to their faces? Middle school boys. Not men. So grow up and be a man.

Here are a couple of ways to cultivate a relationship with your spouse:

Have a date night. I am surprised—shocked, really—by how few church planters have date nights. This is very practical. If you are going to have an affair with someone, you cultivate it by sending flowers or writing notes and seeing each other when you can. Don't fail to do this because you're married!

My parents didn't have a set date night when I was a kid but one of the best things they did for us kids is they would go on vacation without us kids!

"Mom, dad, what are you packing for?"

"We're going on a cruise!"

"Where?"

"The Caribbean!"

"Can I come?"

"Nope."

"Why?"

"Because I'll have more fun without you!"

"You'll have more fun when I'm here with a babysitter I don't like?"

"Yep."

That was a little discouraging. But now I'm married, and a little while back, my wife and I went to New York for the weekend. You know who didn't come? The kids. See ya, suckers!

What are you doing to cultivate a relationship?

Let me add another way that all of you need to cultivate a relationship: **counseling**. We all reach times where we need a third party to listen impartially and speak into our lives. The two common objections to counseling are that you can't afford it or you just don't need it. If you think you don't need counseling you are either arrogant or naïve. The Bible says, "Confess your sins to each other and pray for each other so that you may be healed" (James 5:16). Counseling is a confidential environment with a trusted person where you can do that.

The other objection I hear is that you can't afford it. I never understand this one. You can't afford to have a great marriage? You can't afford to cultivate a relationship with your spouse? You can't afford fulfillment and joy and fun? Getting out of debt is more important than the person you became one with? Having a nice car is more important than having a family you can't wait to see each day?

Cultivate the relationship with your spouse.

Step #3 is to COMPARE your spouse with Christ

When you compare your spouse with other people that's unrealistic. It's reality versus fantasy. You compare your spouse with someone at work who's always dressed nice and presents themselves well and has nice breath. You see your spouse in their pajamas and with their debt and how they eat and with their nasty morning breath. So comparisons are unrealistic.

Instead, find the qualities in your spouse that are Christ-like and, here's the key, *let them know about it.* 1 Thessalonians 5:11 says, "Encourage one another and build each other up, just as in fact you are doing." I have figured one thing out about marriage, and it could be just me and my wife that are like this. Maybe we're different from every other person and couple, though I suspect not. The way I get my wife to do something isn't to point out when she does something wrong; it's to compliment when she does something right.

Maybe a year ago I told my wife that I really appreciate

it when she makes the bed. I never make our bed. I used to think it was a waste of time, but I said, "Honey I really like when you make our bed." She was kind of surprised that I cared, but you know what happens now? Our kids will destroy the entire house (because honestly, a lot of days it seems like that is their goal), but you know what's happened? Our bed looks like something out of a magazine, all made with its 17,000 pillows and everything.

Contrast that to the other day when our bedroom was a wreck and I said, "I'm sick of this; it looks like a college frat house in here." You know what Lindsay did that day? Nothing! I don't know why, but it wasn't quite as motivational.

There are a lot of us who are guilty of nagging our spouse. But that doesn't do anything except make them bitter! Instead, catch them acting like Christ and compliment them on their humility and generosity and hospitality. And you will see more and more of those Christ-like characteristics.

Step #4: Give AFFECTION to your spouse

They need a back rub every now and then! Give them a hug, hold their hand. And men, we need to get better at this because this is a greater need for women than men. One woman said, "I wish my husband would be affectionate with me when he doesn't want something else." I heard another person explain it like this: men need to understand the difference between affection, comma and affection, period. Men, we need to get better at affection, period.

Step #5 is to have SEX with your spouse

1 Corinthians 7:3 says that "the husband should fulfill his marital duty to his wife, and likewise the wife to her husband." Guys, this includes experiencing passion with your spouse. Don't skip straight to sex. Experience passion. You've heard it said women are like crockpots, men are like microwaves. Men, some of you need to slow things down a little bit and bring some passion to your relationship.

Women, some of you need to spice up the passion a little more. Tommy Nelson says the most Christian store at the mall is Victoria's Secret. And there are a bunch of men who want to say Amen right now but they're too scared.

Sex is the number one need of a man in marriage, not just physically but emotionally. I was talking to a friend a few years ago who has several kids and asked how Father's Day was, and he said, "It stunk!" I asked why and he said, "Well, my wife made me a huge, great meal. We went to the park with our kids and had a blast, we watched a good movie, but then we went to bed." I asked why it stunk and he said, "We didn't have sex! Father's day is not a good day if there is no sex involved!"

Step #6 is ACCEPTANCE

Accept that you can have a great marriage. To you singles, accept the fact that God can create a great marriage for you. Don't give up on his plan. Some of you singles are tempted to think you have to sacrifice God's timeline or God's morals. In our pride we want to think: a great marriage is possible and it depends on my spouse—if she's good-looking enough, if he listens well, if he or she makes enough money. But the first step to a great marriage is to kill your pride and believe that a great marriage is possible—and it depends on you. Do you have the humility to speak and act in ways that demonstrate that you believe in your marriage and are going to make this thing work?

And that leads to what I think is the most important of all of these steps:

Step #1 is GRACE.

This is the foundation of a great marriage. See, there are none of us who have been perfect. And there are two kinds of grace: pre-grace and post-grace. Pre-grace is what you decide before someone ever messes up, that you will show them grace. If you enter marriage without pre-grace, that's the first step in having an affair. When we take our vows, we pre-decide, "I know you're going to mess up. And I'm going to offer grace when that happens." It's not easy. It doesn't mean they don't ask for forgiveness. But it's you killing your pride.

And then there's post-grace, because some of you have gone through some or all of these steps towards an affair, and it's been a long time since you've done these steps with your mate.

Jesus said in Mark 10: "At the beginning of creation, God 'made them male and female, and the two will become one flesh.' For this reason a man will leave his father and mother and be united with his wife, and the two will become one flesh. So they are no longer two, but one flesh. Therefore, what God has joined together, let no one separate" (v. 7-9).

Church planting is hard. Going on this journey with a spouse that you are 'one' with makes it much easier. So cultivate a marriage that is a safe place, full of intimacy, and a representation of Christ and his church.

Now let's talk about how churches need to emulate the business world and live out the principles of capitalism that actually will grow the church.

Chapter 9

EMBRACE COMPETITION

Nick Foles contemplated retirement. The quarterback had bounced around NFL teams, and after going 4-7 as a starter with the Rams, and the Rams drafting another quarterback, Foles asked to be released and leaned towards retirement. But the Philadelphia Eagles called and asked him to be their backup, so he agreed. It appeared that he wouldn't play much, as the starting QB, Carson Wentz, was in the discussion for NFL MVP. But then Wentz went down with a season-ending injury, Foles stepped in and ended up leading the Philadelphia Eagles to be Super Bowl LII. (Why does the NFL love Roman numerals? No one knows.) Not only that, Foles was named MVP after throwing for 3 touchdowns and catching another. Once you changed the context, he went from backup with a losing record to Super Bowl MVP. The moral of that story is that sometimes all we need is a new context in which we work to be capable of greater things.

> # The problem today is that church planters are told to fit the mold.

My kids recently got gelatin kits from their grandmother that came with Jell-O and several shaped molds. We ended up with Jell-O stars and moons and planets, and my kids had a great time scarfing down what seemed like a galaxy of sugar created just for them.

Molds are a great thing to use when you're making Jell-O with your kids. However, they're horrible to use when advising someone on how to plant a church.

And here's the thing: it's not what the advisors *say*. They say they want you to use your gifts. They say contextualize the Gospel. They say to investigate the culture and plant accordingly. But the unfortunate reality is that while they say many of the right things, they subtly communicate something else.

Have you ever encountered someone who has Asperger's Syndrome? Most (but not all) of the people with this condition cannot understand sarcasm. They can't interpret tone or hyperbole, so they take what you say exactly at face value. Literally. It's often difficult to communicate accurately with someone who has Asperger's because you don't even realize how much you use sarcasm or intonation, or even simply metaphors, to communicate things. It ends up being embarrassing for you and frustrating for the person who can't understand you.

What happens in church planting is that the planter takes his organization's words at face value and set out to plant a new kind of church. But then he gets corrected: You can't do it that way. Our denomination needs to know this specific statistic. We don't want you to spend money on that. The church planter ends up frustrated by being put into that box, the leading organization feels the planter is trying to usurp its authority, and the bottom line is the local church suffers because energy is taken away from the church so that everyone can get on the same page.

> # You need to get to a point where you don't know what can't be done.

Embrace Competition

There is no question that competition brings out the best in certain people. Athletes, salespeople, and politicians all spring to mind when we talk about the benefits of competition. However, almost no one applies the same principle to church, which I think is a big mistake. In the church world, we're told that competition is bad, that we're here to save everyone, and that we're all on the same team.

But when I took the famous StrengthsFinder test, do

you know what my number one strength was? Competition. And I had a kind of crisis of identity when I first read that. The first thought that went through my brain was, "Well, duh," but immediately after that, I thought, "Wait. If I want to be a church planter, and churches aren't supposed to be competitive, but my greatest strength is competition, does that mean I shouldn't be a church planter?"

Of course not! Every strength is a gift from God that can and should be used for his glory, even competition! And not just in athletes, whom we naturally assume gain from it, but also in teachers and doctors and firefighters, and even church planters. I knew I was called to plant a church, I knew that God was leading me that direction, and now I knew that competition was my greatest strength. I had three options: 1) Give up on being a church planter because competition doesn't fit the mold of church, 2) plant a church but mitigate my greatest strength the whole way, no matter what, or 3) find a healthy way to put this gift to use to plant the best church possible.

I started by learning how to compete against the healthiest target: myself. This is why numbers started to become so important to me in my ministry. They not only tell stories and give God glory, but they also give me a benchmark against which to compare myself and the organization I have led in building. So I started there. This motivated me, brought out the best in me, and really helped to focus the gift God gave me for his glory.

Conventional wisdom talks out of both sides of its mouth. In one breath, it says to use your gifts, but in the next, it says, "only if your gifts fit into this specific church mold." If I had followed that advice, I would either have quit or else tried my best to hide my greatest gift by pretending to be someone I wasn't.

I decided instead to follow the contrarian way, which is this: **Use your gifts to create your own mold.**

At over 60 million copies sold, the best selling book of all time is *The Purpose Driven Church* by Rick Warren, the pastor of Saddleback Church in California. The book is fantastic, and it led a lot of churches to do a lot of good in a lot of ways in a lot of places. However, one of the fallouts was that a massive number of churches started trying not only to follow the principles in Warren's book, but also to mimic some of the more specific practices, policies, and procedures of Rick Warren's church. Saddleback did it a certain way for reasons that made sense in its context, but other churches would try to carbon copy that into their own church with its own context, leading to a haphazard application of programming instead of a wholehearted application of principles.

You see, what works in one church won't necessarily work in another church for a whole host of reasons. The audience is different, so you can't preach the same way. The locals have a different background with church, so you can't evangelize the same way. The movers and shakers don't make the same amount of money, so you can't fundraise the same way. The property is a significantly different price and type, so you can't even construct a building the same way. (Compare property prices in Howard County, Maryland, against those in Escambia County, Florida, for example, and you'll see my point.)

But most importantly, the pastor is different, so you

can't lead the same way as other pastors. The conventional wisdom has this idealized version of the pastor that puts potential church planters through a meat grinder so they all come out the same: dressing the same, talking the same, leading the same. But the conventional wisdom is not only wrong; it goes against what we know about God from the Bible. God doesn't just call people who already fit a certain mold. We see that over and over again in Scripture. If anything, we see the opposite: God anointing people into His service who so radically are outside the mold that no one takes them seriously. You see, God doesn't call the already molded.

> # God calls people, and then He molds them according to his purpose.

And because that purpose isn't identical for every church in every circumstance, pastors ought to be as diverse in their personalities, preaching styles, and leadership as the communities they serve. It does no good for a church planter built to lead from his competitiveness to try to lead from his empathy if that's not his strength. Even though empathy is something people say they want in their pastor, they would rather have a pastor who's real and says that isn't him than one who fakes empathy because he and others think he should look like that.

This principle doesn't just apply to pastors, though; it

applies to churches as a whole. While it was a really good thing for churches to shift from formal Sunday attire to more casual clothes so that people could come as they were and not feel judged, there are certain places where this is not fully appropriate. If your church is planted in one of the oldest areas in the country, this makes no sense! Those people are highly likely to show up in more formal wear, and so should you because they may not take your message about Jesus seriously otherwise. By dressing casually, you would be creating an unnecessary off-ramp away from Jesus. On the other hand, if your primary audience is 20- to 30-year-olds, a suit and tie with a pocket watch is more like to turn them off than to invite them towards Jesus, and by "dressing your best for God," you would have led people away from Him.

This simple demonstration about clothing illustrates the larger point: **You Do You.** It makes no sense to try to be someone you're not. It's ingenuine, which is already a non-starter for most people, and you'll find yourself working against your own grain to accomplish things that would go much more smoothly and easily if you weren't trying to conform to some master mold of pastoring that you think you should fit into.

I think this is where a lot of the tension of what church should be breaks down. Follow your gifts! If you are best at preaching, build a church around that. If you are best at one-on-one discipleship, craft your model around that.

> # The contrarian church planter recognizes that the ideal church will never be planted.

So we've got to plant one that uses our gifts. Someone once put it this way: "I like the way I'm doing church better than the way you're not doing it." Here are some key reasons to employ your gifts rather than trying to fit the mold.

Reason #1: Demographics are Important

In his book *Microtrends*, Mark Penn explains that in the last fifteen years, we have seen the fragmentation of the United States. Penn ran the presidential election campaign from Bill Clinton and coined the term "soccer moms." He notes that different tribes are forming in our country. Consider the following from his research:

- Only 31 percent of US households have children, and that number is declining.
- About 1.5 million children in the US between the ages of 8 and 18 are vegetarians, up from virtually zero fifty years ago.
- The US Census reports that in recent years, the number of households with no English speakers has risen 50 percent to over 12 million people.

- The fastest growing sports in the last ten years are skateboarding, kayaking, snowboarding, and archery.
- Homeschool students now outnumber charter school and voucher students combined.

The bottom line of these statistics is that there are tens of thousands of different fragments in our society that could have churches targeted just to that demographic. Why do we think the church needs to look the same in every context? It can, and must, look different if we are to reach more people with the hope of Christ.

Reason #2: Differences are Good

I once told another planter that I didn't think any city had enough churches. He wisely corrected me, "No, Carl, no city has enough *different* churches." One reason I like the multisite phenomenon is that it will force different kinds of churches to be planted. Think about it: if your city gets its own site of a Life Church or a North Point, you won't be able to plant a church by copying and pasting their mold. You will be forced to plant a unique church. This is a good thing! We need not just new churches but new styles, new philosophies, new experiences with ways to reach new people with the old Gospel.

The Practical Stuff

Now that I've (hopefully) convinced you not to fit into the mold, what on earth *should* you do. While I can't necessarily answer that question universally, here's some of the wisdom I've gleaned from my practice as a contrarian church planter.

Advice #1: Don't try to look like other pastors look

I assume you've felt the tension. You're wired a certain way, but you see other pastors do certain things and use certain phrases, and it looks effective there, so why not here? Why not do what they're doing and look how they're looking?

I took a team of lay leaders to a church planting conference recently. The first night, I asked them what stood out to them so far. The first two guys shared things they had learned in the various sessions and assemblies, but the third guy pointed out, "I feel like I need to go buy a trendy shirt that has needless buttons on the top of it."

Many denominations are experiencing a shortage of pastors; they have more churches than they do leaders. I believe this is one of the main reasons why. If we communicate that all pastors have to fit into a certain mold, we're missing a lot of people who would be great church leaders. They think—precisely because we've demonstrated it to them—that pastors have to act, look, and lead a certain way.

As contrarians, we have to release ourselves from that expectation.

Advice #2: Come up with a "not to do" list

Make a list of things that you will *not* do, and clearly communicate them to your church. One application in my life is that I don't do counseling. Zerp. Nada. Zilch. I say this from time to time in sermons so people don't expect it from me. It's not because I don't care about people or think that counseling isn't valuable. (It is!) It's that in reality, I'm a horrible, absolutely no good counselor. If I counsel people, I'll want to talk the whole time, clean everything up nicely as quickly as possible, and be too direct with answers instead of asking good questions. That's just who I am! So I have a list of professional counselors I refer people to whenever I hear about someone who needs professional help.

But really, it's in everyone's best interest that I don't do counseling, and not just because I'm bad at it. If I tried to focus on counseling, which isn't my area of giftedness, because "that's what pastors do," I'd be stealing time away from my actual areas of giftedness, preaching, and leadership. And if I don't put real time there, I wouldn't do those as well, meaning that the things God created me to do wouldn't be done with excellence. In that scenario, nobody benefits. The couple who needed counseling doesn't benefit because they get a crappy counselor (me). I don't benefit because I would feel trapped in something I'm not good at. My staff doesn't benefit because I'm not spending time working on leading them well. My weekend audience doesn't benefit because I'm not focusing on preaching to them with excellence. And God doesn't really benefit because instead of focusing on what He's called and built me to do, which He meant to bring His lost children home, I'm spending an hour on something He didn't mean for me to be doing in the first place. Nobody wins!

Now, it's important to note that the motivation behind your not-to-do list must be humble and serving of others.

This should come from a passion for effectiveness, not arrogance or avoidance. If setting up portable church is on your not-to-do list just because you don't like doing that, you're thinking too highly about yourself. No servant is above his master. Jesus washed your feet; you can set up pipe and drape.

But if an item is on your list because you have raised other people to lead in that area and because it's better for you to spend more time in prayer or with your sermon, that's a good thing. A not-to-do list isn't saying you're too good for something; it's saying that it's not the best use of your time. If you refuse to do those things, you may be arrogant, but if you've put other people in place to do them, you may be wise.

Advice #3: Write your own job description

This is where you get super practical. Actually, physically write down your own job description. Not just an ideal one, not one that fits everyone else's expectations, and not one that puts you above anyone else. But a real one. One that fits your actual gifts, your church's true needs, and God's perfect calling on your life.

I believe your job description should have three things.

1. **The things they pay you to do.** Bottom line is that there are some things they have to pay you to do. Maybe it's responding to an email or following up with visitors. Maybe it's something else. But for every pastor there's a list of things that you don't want to do, that you're not great at, but because you are the lead pastor you have to do them.

2. **The necessary things you'd do for free.** These are the required parts of your jobs that you absolutely love to do. This could be writing sermons or meeting with new visitors for coffee. Whatever in your job that is necessary for the church and that you deeply enjoy doing goes here.

3. **Things that are outside the box.** This is where you step back and say, "What are the things that I am uniquely wired to do that can make this church better at its mission?" Perhaps this is developing a new way to reach the lost or thinking long-term big-picture about the lasting legacy of your church.

Those three items are so important because they focus on what's necessary and not just what people expect or what you think a "real pastor" would do. The point is to put your God-given gifts to work for His kingdom so that more and more people can come to experience the life-changing grace of Jesus.

Chapter 10

YOUR CHURCH DOESN'T NEED
LEBRON JAMES

"The block." That's what they called it. It was Game 7 of the 2016 NBA finals, pitting LeBron James' Cavaliers against Steph Curry's Warriors. With less than 2 minutes remaining, I watched in awe as LeBron raced down the court, chasing Golden State forward Andre Iguodala from behind and seemingly came from nowhere to block his layup attempt.

LeBron James is arguably the best basketball player of all time. As of this writing, he's competed in almost 1100 games, scored almost 30,000 points, and won three national championships, placing him among the all-time greats.

A little while back, LeBron played a game at a position he doesn't normally play. He's usually a power forward, a position for which he's perfectly suited. But in this game, his coach decided to play him at small forward, which has a completely different function and role in the game plan.

How did LeBron do? He scored 34 points, that's how.

So what happened? Was there some clever coaching scheme afoot? Should LeBron have been playing that position the whole time? What's going on? A reporter decided to ask, and LeBron answered with simply this: he's known and practiced every play for every position since he was a kid. Because of that muscle memory, playing small forward for him felt no different than playing power forward, and he went on dominate the game.

That's pretty darn impressive. It's the kind of performance that makes you want to go and pastor like LeBron plays, able and nimble no matter what comes your way and being perfectly suited for every possible scenario.

But let's be real: LeBron is a freak. Maybe one player in a generation is that naturally gifted. For him to be so capable at different positions is exceptionally rare, even among other all-time great players. Maybe, just maybe, there's a pastor out there somewhere in the world who is just like that, performing all kinds of tasks and filling every role with exquisite talent and precision, holding the full range of gifts and abilities. Maybe.

But you're almost certainly not that guy. I know I'm not. So it's time we stopped acting like it, for two reasons:

First, we will not grow in the necessary gifts if we nurture gifts outside our role. I'm an above average creative director. I did it at a church for years before I planted Mosaic. One might think that I have a significant role in running our creative department now, but I don't. I've given that whole department away to other people. I barely even touch it. Why? Because by spending time on creative arts, I would be taking time away from preparing to preach and leading my church. As the pastor, my role requires those functions, but it doesn't require me to manage the creative department. Sure, I *could* do it, but that would subtract the amount of time, energy, and heart I have left to focus on what my position actually requires.

Second, our church will only grow to the extent that we let it. To use the same example, let's pretend that I did have the time, energy, and passion left over to run the creative department. That sure would be efficient and require less staff oversight, freeing them up to do other things. It might even eliminate a staff position, saving the church money! But just think about how many fewer people would grow if I did that. There are the leaders who would back off when they saw me engage. There are the volunteers who would never feel like they could rise up and lead because there I would be blocking the way. And then there's the staff member who could truly do an amazing job leading this department, but I've either limited his authority or even eliminated his position! By being hands-on here, I've actually stunted my church's growth, but by sticking to my position, by not pretending to be LeBron James (which I'm definitely not), I not only grow more in the ways my church needs me to, but I also let my church grow into their roles as well.

Larry Osborne has talked about how church staffs grow from being a golf foursome to a basketball team to a football team. In a golf foursome, everyone plays together a lot, they all know each other's styles and idiosyncrasies, and they work on many of the same elements together. For a basketball team, the positions are somewhat more specialized, but they all generally work on the same plays together, even if they all have different roles. (A short point guard isn't going to play center!) And then there are football teams, which are so large and specialized that many players don't even know each other, much less work on the same things. How often does a linebacker practice with the running back? Pretty much never. It's entirely possible they've never even met.

For the lead pastor, this principle is important to learn because there are three temptations each pastor might face in regards to his position on the team:

1. Insecurity

This is the pastor who won't lead because he thinks that leading and taking charge and casting the vision makes him look arrogant. This isn't humility; this is hesitancy. Every army needs a general; every country needs a president; every team needs a coach. When the lead pastor doesn't take charge, everyone suffers. Everyone loses. What the insecure pastor must do is realize that his decisiveness and leadership doesn't stem from who he is, but from the mission. God doesn't call him to be correct; God calls him to be commander.

2. Arrogance

This is the pastor who thinks he *does* know what to do in all situations. He believes he's the smartest person in the room. He enjoys people knowing he's the lead pastor, and he hates having his opinions and decisions questioned. What the arrogant pastor must realize is that that the only thing we know for sure is the Gospel. Everything else is educated guesswork. If this pastor will admit when he's wrong and confess that he doesn't actually know all that much, it will paradoxically *increase* people's trust in him because they'll know that the only thing that ultimately matters is the Gospel of grace.

3. Laziness

Steven Sample wrote a fantastic book called *Contrarian's Guide to Leadership.* (Sound familiar?) In that book, he talks about the first time he became president of a university. He was at Indiana University, had just been named president, and was walking across campus when he ran into a professor. The picture I got when hearing this story is that the professor was one of those old crusty types who'd been around forever because he loved to teach. He congratulated Sample, but then--with a look in his eye as if he was remembering specific people--said, "Steven, let me give you some advice. Some people want to BE president. Some want to DO president." And then he walked away.

Sample goes on to talk about how lots of people want the benefits of *being* president: the salary, the notoriety, the private jet. But few want the responsibility--the constant fundraising, always being on the clock, dealing with policies or drama that cause problems. He realized success is found in doing president.

Some people want to be pastor, but don't want to do pastor. This person thinks that volunteers and staff exist to serve him. He doesn't do things he doesn't like to do. He'll use good leadership principles like "do what only you can do" to justify laziness. But the reality is that he's living out a bad leadership principle: "do what only you *want* to do." What the lazy pastor must do is, first of all, repent. After that, even though it seems simplistic, he needs to make sure he's doing something each week that he doesn't want to do. For me, I do two things to remind myself each week that I'm a pastor and not a CEO.

First, I stand in the lobby after each service to talk, meet, and pray with people. I'm an introvert. I'd rather go hide in my office. But one time, I was with a pastor named Jim Burgen, and I asked him why, at his church of then 15,000, he stood in the lobby after each service. He looked at me like I was an idiot and said, "Because I don't want to be *that* guy!" I nodded as if to say, "Well....*I* knew that. I just wanted to make sure *you* knew that!" But ever since, I've stood in the lobby after every service.

The other thing I do each week that I don't want to do is write some handwritten notes to volunteers to thank them, and you know what? I *hate* writing them. It's tedious. I often don't know the people I'm writing them to. I wonder if the recipients even care. But I do this for the same reason: I don't want to be *that* guy, the pastor who's so full of himself that he disconnects from the very people God had commissioned him to serve and lead.

The reason I go into these three temptations is that if you don't address these things, you'll never evolve into your role or grow as a leader. You'll be stuck in a small-minded framework for leadership that will ultimately prevent you and your church from growing.

Once you understand who you are and are comfortable in your own skin, it will become easier to grow into your role. The tricky part is that you don't evolve from golf foursome to basketball team to football team in one day, one year, or often even one decade. But first, a few cautions.

Don't be too quick to jump to the next level.

All change is hard, even good change. Most growing pains are healthy, but they're still pain. So unlike most leadership, you'd rather err on the side of waiting too long to act like a basketball team than do it too early. I can speak to this from experience. We spent years as a foursome but rapidly became a football team over a short period of time. It ended up hurting people on our team, and we had to backtrack.

Don't make decisions you know you shouldn't make.

Again, as the adage says, "do what only you can do." Hopefully, there was a time in your life where you were not the lead pastor, so you remember what it was like when your leader made a decision that annoyed you, not because it was necessarily wrong but simply because it was a decision *you* should have made because that was your role at the time and not his. If you have good people, *let them lead*. And if you don't have good people, *let them lead* because the only way they'll grow is through trial! Some lead pastors keep all the decisions to themselves, and it hinders their ultimate goal of growing the church to reach people for Christ because people quickly realize that he's not a leader. He's a dictator!

Do make decisions that you should make.

This goes back to the insecurity we discussed earlier, but the principle is clear: sometimes you, and only you, can make a decision for your church. One thing my staff told me once has really stuck with me: **"Carl, we don't need you to be right, but we do need you to be clear."**

> "In any moment of decision, the best thing you can do is the right thing, the next best thing is the wrong thing, and the worst thing you can do is nothing."
> -Theodore Roosevelt-

People crave a clear vision. Give it to them. As lead pastor, you're the only person who can do this. We often look up to other pastors as an example of what we want to do in ministry, but most of the time we follow the wrong examples. I don't mean you chose the wrong pastor to emulate; I mean that we chose the wrong thing about those pastors to emulate. You copied the WHAT and not the HOW of their ministry, so you end up starting the same program or preaching the same way as whoever your particular pastor crush is.

A better way to lead is to ask *how* they got there, not what they are doing. How did they arrive at those systems? How do they think? If you answer all those questions, you'll still be yourself, but you'll have learned the deeper things that made that pastor successful.

Speaking of clear vision, sometimes you're going to have strong opinions about small things. This is normal. This is okay. This can even be good. The little things matter a great deal. If you have such an opinion, say so! People want clarity from you, and the worst thing in the world is for you to get frustrated because you stayed quiet about something that really bothers you. That will only upset the person because they thought they were leading well, but really you had just not provided enough direction.

I have made an official ban of glitter at all Mosaic related activities. I know: you probably think, "Any rational person would do the same." But I instituted the ban once upon a time after an event had glitter and we found it on the chairs the next week...and the week after that...and the week after that...you get my point. (By the way, I did point out to my staff the recent article entitled: "Scientists Call for Global Glitter Ban." I was ahead of my time.)

Since we're talking about roles, here's something we should clear up.

You are not the most important person in your church.

You're not even close. I know it seems that way. You make most of the decisions; the authority seems to come from you; you're the one who started the place. You're the singularity, right? Wrong. That role doesn't belong to you even remotely. Your role is to lead, that's true, but Jesus has already said who it is that builds His church: Him, and no one else. "On this rock *I* will build my church" (Matthew 16:18, emphasis mine). Not a denomination, not a strategy, not an organization, and definitely not YOU. Jesus will build the church, and no one else.

So what's your role? Is it leader or follower?

It's both. Your job is to lead people *in* following. You're not the primary leader; that's Jesus. You're the first follower. You're the guy saying, "Jesus is awesome, and His way of doing things leads to eternal life and a better life right now. We should follow Him!" In that role, you have to lead, you have to organize, you have to construct. But you're not the founder of the church, or even of your church. You're there because Jesus is Lord over all, and you have to act like it.

That means not being arrogant and assuming you have all the answers. That means not being insecure and thinking your decisions aren't good enough. And that means not being lazy and treating others as beneath you. To lead in Christ's church, you have to be the first follower, the first servant, and the first submitter.

Work Like An Arminian, Sleep Like a Calvinist

For the last several centuries, there has always been a debate over the Christian beliefs of Arminianism and Calvinism. It's a whole big thing that mostly amounts to Christians shouting over each other and generally just creating a lot of unnecessary noise. Pastors and theologians go around asking each other which camp they're in, which parts of TULIP they agree or disagree with and how much, and if there's free will then how God's sovereignty works.

Those debates are good and all, and there's merit to both sides. I can see definitive Scriptural backing for each of them and for a lot of positions in between. Practically speaking, however, I have a philosophy when it comes to pastoral ministry: **I work like an Arminian and sleep like a Calvinist**.

Here's what I mean. You've probably heard the term "Protestant work ethic." It came after the Reformation, of course, when predestination theology became popular as a belief and a conversation. An outgrowth of this idea was that because people were either predestined or not, and it was impossible to know which, then maybe you could tell who was "elect" by observing their way of life. In other words, if someone was saved, their actions would necessarily change, and you could "see" whether they were really saved or not.

So the result was that people who were following Jesus worked harder because they wanted to prove that they were saved. The irony here, of course, is that the Reformation accurately rebelled against a works-based salvation, but an unintentional result was that practically, many people worked harder to prove that they had received a non-works-based salvation!

I say I want to work like an Arminian because I don't want to work to prove that I'm saved, but I do want to be known by a strong work ethic regardless. At the same time, I want to sleep like a Calvinist. When I lay my head on my pillow each night, I want to *know* that God is in complete control, that He cares about His church more even than I do. I want to fall asleep in God's grace and provision, knowing and believing in His providence.

Never fall for the false dichotomy forcing you to pick a "side." Rather, embrace the idea that both "sides" have merits from which you can learn how to better follow God's will, and they each have flaws to avoid as you carry out your mission. This hybrid understanding of planting is essential to my strategy for growing our church, and I think it will work for you, too. Rather than dogmatically living in just one camp of thinking, I have asserted, and will continue to assert, that living out the best qualities of both is the true secret to success in leading God's church.

Speaking of secrets, the next chapter is one that you'll definitely want to read.

Chapter 11

BECOME A PROUD BIBLE NERD

One of the best movies ever is *Hoosiers*. Seriously. If you disagree with me, repent so we can move on. And if you haven't seen the movie, put down this book and go start watching. (Because I'm going to ruin the end. Hey, it's been out for longer than you've been alive; get over it!) *Hoosiers* is based on a true story and follows the boys' basketball team from small, rural Hickory High School in 1952. They get a new coach (Gene Hackman) and under his leadership become a great team.

The end of the movie culminates with the statewide basketball tournament. Keep in mind this was back when there weren't different divisions for high school sports, so they're a tiny school going against all the bigger schools in the entire state. They have lots of dramatic moments, where every member of the team contributes in some way to a string of victories (even underhanded shooting Ollie!) and they make it to the state final.

One of the best scenes in the movie is before the state final. These boys from a small farm team walk into the empty arena where they will play the championship the next day. Their mouths drop open in awe of the big arena. You can see them getting nervous. But what unfolds next is what we need to remember as church planters.

Coach Dale (Hackman) pulls out a tape measure and says, "Bill, measure how far it is to the free throw line." The answer: 15 feet. Then he says, "Measure how high the rim is." 10 feet. "Just like back home boys."

His point was so simple: *What got us here will get us there.* The same basketball that won the sectional will win us the championship. Sure enough, the star player Jimmy hits a buzzer beater, and Hickory wins the championship.

What Coach Dale reminded his team of his what I often need reminding of in ministry. I pray that as you plant your church, it grows. I pray that you experience success and move into bigger venues, baptize more people, and expose more guests to the Gospel every year. But the thing we must remember if we are to continue doing what we set out to do is this: no matter how big or small we get, it's the same game.

I first learned this several years ago. I was listening to a leadership podcast by a megachurch pastor from Texas, and he was talking about growth. He said that because his church is on all those biggest church lists and because their budget is tens of millions of dollars per year, someone asked him, "Do you feel more pressure now than you used to?" His answer: No way! He went on to explain, "I feel the same pressure as always. Sure, our numbers have more zeroes, but it's still lost people we're trying to reach. So the pressure hasn't changed."

That taught me that the same foundation that you build on is the same thing you build with, which leads me to this contrarian principle: **Stay grounded in God's word.**

I know, I know, I know. as soon as you read that you want to skip this chapter. I get it! Here's why. The whole reason you bought this book is that you are looking for something else to help you. And I think you should be committed to becoming a lifelong learner, so I commend you for getting this far. In addition, I'm the same as you are. I want to learn everything I can from anyone I can so I can accomplish everything I can for God's kingdom. So if going to a conference helps me reach the lost, I'm in. If reading a book helps, I'll do it. If attending a seminar will help, let's go.

And it doesn't stop there. I agree with Craig Groeschel, who said, "I will do everything short of sin in order to reach the lost." So if having haze in our service helps reach the lost, let's do it. If changing our graphics package will engage the lost, I'm on board. If doing that song or not doing that song or having that type of band, or that level of music volume, or wearing that style of clothes, or having this service time, or whatever else helps reach the lost, I'm following Jesus in doing those things.

But here's my temptation...in my zeal for learning the latest greatest methods, I forget the foundation. So I have caught myself at times spending more time thinking about lighting or t-shirts or catchphrases than I spend thinking about how to communicate God's word to hurting people.

***

When I was in college one of my part-time jobs was working on the grounds crew on campus. Typically that meant mowing lawns and mulching flower beds. But one particular day we got in the truck and drove over to a house that our college owned adjacent to campus. Picture an old house that was ornate, massive, and gorgeous. My boss told us that our job was to go through the house and take out anything that could be salvaged: light fixtures, plumbing fixtures, anything, because it was scheduled for demolition the following week.

I couldn't believe that our school was going to tear down such an old, beautiful building. So I asked my boss why this was happening, and he gave a simple explanation: "The foundation is ruined. It's beyond being fixed, so it's not safe. The only safe thing to do is to bulldoze the entire house."

I've seen the same thing happen to churches.

There are actually entire denominations today that are dying because they got away from the Bible. Decades ago they were reaching the lost, serving the community, and providing hope for many people. But today they are dying, because they started focusing on the wrong things, and their foundation crumbled underneath them.

I actually drive by one of these churches every day on my way home from church. It's part of a denomination that used to number in the tens of millions in our country alone. The church building I see is beautiful on the outside, but most weeks I can count on two hands the number of cars in the parking lot. That's what happens when you get away from the Bible as your foundation. Many of the things we can get distracted by as church leaders are important. But if they ultimately distract us from the Bible, our foundation is crumbling.

I've told you I'm into data. Let me show you some data. An organization compiled multiple studies and here's what they found:

- Reading the Bible 4+ times per week decreases your odds of giving in to these temptations:
    - Drinking to excess -62%
    - Viewing pornography -59%
    - Having sex outside marriage -59%
    - Lashing out in anger -31%
    - Gossiping – 28%
    - Neglecting family -26%
    - Overeating or mishandling food -20%
    - Mishandling money -20%
- Reading the Bible 4+ times per week decreases your odds of struggling with these issues:
    - Feeling bitter -40%
    - Thinking destructively about yourself -32%
    - Feeling like you have to hide what you do or feel -32%
    - Having difficulty forgiving others -31%
    - Feeling discouraged -31%
    - Experiencing loneliness – 30%
    - Experiencing fear or anxiety -14%

Translation: Even if you don't' believe in Jesus—if you are lonely or if you don't want to hurt yourself, get in

Scripture every day! But it keeps going. Think of these stats as a church leader.

- Reading the Bible 4+ times per week gives you significantly higher odds of:
    - Giving financially to a church +416%
    - Discipling others +231%
    - Sharing your faith with others +228%
- Reading the Bible 4+ times per week gives you significantly lower odds of:
    - Feeling spiritually stagnant -60%
    - Feeling like you can't please God -44%

Lifeway Research sums it up well: "Reading the Bible is the number one predictor of spiritual maturity." Here's the thing: those stats are all about personal reading. But how are people going to start reading the Bible daily? It's simple: by you teaching them.

> # The #1 best habit a church planter can have is daily time in the Bible.

I know what you're thinking: "This is supposed to be the *contrarian's* guide to church planting. How come we're talking about a basic spiritual discipline?" Here's why: because most church planters aren't in the Word every day.

We say we want to grow; we say we want to reach the lost; we SAY lots of things. But our actions (says the book of James) show what we really believe. And the data shows that if you want to follow Christ and experience true life through him, getting in the Word is the path to do that.

A couple years ago I did something unique: I tried to read the Bible in just ninety days. I think I made it in about one hundred. Either way, I was reading bigger chunks of the Bible in a day than I've ever done before or since. There are some disadvantages to that, but there are also some advantages, including the fact that you get the big picture of Scripture very well.

During this time I became pretty annoyed with Scripture for a bit, here's why: it kept repeating the same story over and over! So you read in Genesis about God choosing Abraham, then you read in Exodus about being delivered from slavery, and the rest of the Torah shows Israel's sin but God bringing them to the Promised Land anyway. Here was my problem: they kept telling that same story over and over and over and over. So that same story is recounted in Joshua...then Judges. It's mentioned by Samuel. It's talked about nonstop in the Psalms, and by the time you get to the prophets, it seems every other chapter at least references that same story. Even the New Testament talks about that same old story.

I was trying to stay engaged enough to get through the Bible in ninety days, so I'm thinking, "Get a new story already! Don't talk about your ancestors, talk about what God is doing today and now!" And then it hit me: **When they remembered how God had been faithful to them in**

the past, they were faithful to God in the present. But when they forgot how God was faithful to them in the past, they were unfaithful to him in the present. In fact, in a time of great unfaithfulness, the Scriptures are discovered and brought to King Josiah, and he doesn't even know what they say!

This is why in Psalm 77 when Asaph is battling spiritual depression, he says, "This is my fate; the Most High has turned his has against me." But then he says, "But then I recall all you have done, O Lord; I remember your wonderful deeds of long ago," and that sets him on the right track again.

Deuteronomy 17 lays out an interesting practice. It says that several generations after the Hebrews enter the Promised Land they will ask for a king. And when that happens, one thing the king must first do is copy down the entire Torah, in his own hand. Then he is to keep that copy of the Law nearby and read from it every single day. The goal, says Scripture, is that he will stay committed to the Lord his entire lifetime. In fact, look at the exact wording: "This regular reading will prevent him from becoming proud and acting as if he is above his fellow citizens. It will also prevent him from turning away from these commands in the smallest way." (Deut 17:20a)

I love that passage because you and I are no different. If we neglect daily reading of God's Word, we will forget that what got us here will get us there, then the foundation will crumble beneath us, and we'll wake up one day wondering what happened.

Everything we're talking about in this chapter is why I

think the most important parable for pastors, and for church planters specifically, is the parable of the sower. I referenced it earlier, but think about how we normally preach and teach this parable. You know the story. The guy throws seed on good soil, on rocky soil, and on the path among thorns, but only the seed on good soil grows. I'm no farmer, but it makes sense to me. But the way preachers always taught this to me would be to explain it and then ask: "What is the soil of your heart? Are you tilling the ground of your heart to make it open to God's word?" And I do believe that's a good question.

But that's not the main point of the parable. The main point of the parable is this: **Have faith in the seed.** It would've been foolish in the story Jesus told for the farmer to say, "Well, this isn't growing on rocky soil. I guess I better try to plant....marbles, or....sticks, or.....whatever!" Jesus' main point in this parable is to keep planting the seed. Don't give up on it! The seed is the Word of God. We've already seen the data. When the seed is planted, it grows.

But the parable also illustrates that when the seed isn't growing, don't beat yourself up, don't blame yourself, don't think there's something wrong with the seed. See, Jesus is simply warning us church leaders: some people will reject it. Some will walk away. Some will leave the faith. And that's okay. Not it's not okay in the sense that it doesn't matter and you shouldn't grieve when someone walks away. But it's okay as in your job isn't to make sure they receive it; your job is to scatter seed by preaching the word of God.

If you get this, you will be free from the tyranny of the

numbers. I specifically put this chapter later than the when I said numbers matter because too many church planters want to act like numbers don't matter. Baloney. However, I don't get the luxury of determining what soil I get to scatter seed in.

The reason this parable is so key for church planters is that there's lots of good stuff out there on being a missionary in your context, and loving the unlovable, and strategies for church planting, and how to do all sorts of things that Christians and the church and church planters need to do. But if you don't scatter the seed of God's word, things won't grow!

So let me end this chapter with 2 specific challenges, one of which I've already briefly hit on.

First, Be in God's word every day

It starts with you. If you want the benefits of all those stats I listed earlier, you have to be the example. You are the "king" from Deuteronomy 17, meaning that if you are in God's word every day, it will impact everyone under your authority in whether they follow God or not.

To be honest, the main reason I used to neglect this was I didn't have a good system. But I took a cue from a Mark Batterson book and put a Bible in my bathroom. (Warning: TMI ahead!) Now, every single day when I wake up, the first thing I do is go in my bathroom, sit down, and I don't get up until I've read the Bible that day. Sometimes I'll read the Bible in a year, sometimes a Psalm a day, sometimes other things. The important thing is that I'm in God's word for him to shape me and speak to me.

Out of that flows a question I ask when I meet with people in our church: "In the last seven days, how many days have you read the Bible?" I don't ask longer than that because people don't remember. But they generally have a good idea of how many days of the last seven they've been in God's word. And I don't ask it in a gotcha-you're-in-trouble-if-it's-not--seven   way.   It's   just   a   simple accountability, and I follow it up with: "What has God been teaching you?" That leads to great conversations and mutual growth.

Preach God's word faithfully

Again, I know what you're thinking: "This is ministry 101; why include this here?" The answer: because most church planters don't preach God's word faithfully! Most church planters go to one of two extremes: they either are so concerned about getting doctrine right that their sermons are boring and irrelevant, or they are so concerned with growing their church that they water it down every so slightly. Often, more than slightly.

You've heard of the extreme diets out there, right?

- There's the cotton ball diet. You dip cotton balls in orange juice and eat them.
- There's the lemonade diet, where you eat nothing but lemonade for 10 days!
- There's the feeding tube diet, where a healthy person gets a feeding tube that feeds them no more than 800 calories a day for 10 days.
- Then there's the tapeworm diet, where you swallow a capsule full of tapeworm eggs. The only downside

besides organ damage is they can live inside you for 30 years!

Back to the subject at hand--I think a lot of church planters feed their churches weird diets. The bottom line is you shouldn't avoid any major healthy food group. Sure, if your goal is to look healthy, I guess you can eat cotton balls and you'll be skinny, and everyone will look at you and think you look good. But the reality is that on the inside you're not healthy because you're neglecting valuable nutrients your body needs, and it's only a matter of time before that hurts you.

That's why I adopted the Bob Russell sermon planning approach. Very practically, here's what he taught me (with a few adaptations) to include in my sermon calendar every year:

- One series based on a part of the Gospels, so maybe a series through the Sermon on the Mount, or a series on parables of Jesus.
- One apologetics series, to both address the skeptic and equip the believer.
- One money series, because consumerism is arguably the biggest sin in our culture. If people get their money right with God, their hearts follow, says Jesus.
- One series from the Old Testament. Typically this is a series on a specific character, for example, a series on the life of Samson.
- One relationship series per year. This could be on marriage, dating, or friendship.

- One series from a New Testament epistle. So this could be going through the book of Philippians and talking about suffering, or it could be going through Romans 8 and letting the text drive the topics.
- One wisdom series per year. You've heard me talk about wisdom a lot. Faith without wisdom can be directionless, so we need God's wisdom to follow him on a daily basis.

For me personally, even when I'm not doing a text-driven sermon, it's still expository in nature in that I pick one central Scripture that drives the day, while sprinkling in other supporting and relevant Scriptures.

One reason I like some expository series, such as the Gospels series or the epistle series, is that it forces me to preach on things I may not otherwise preach on. This is one area church planters get in trouble because we want to grow the crowd, so you might avoid hard topics or Scriptures. But let me remind you: God has chosen you to lead this thing, and he has given you his word. Your job is to be a chef and serve the bread of life in a way that helps people.

For example, a few years ago I was preaching through an epistle and got to a section on slavery. I thought, "how in the world does this apply to today?" Then I remembered multiple conversations with skeptical nonbelievers who say, "How can you even believe the Bible when it endorses slavery?" So I preached a sermon called "Is the Bible racist and outdated?" I used that section as my text. I walked people through what slavery was at different points in the Bible, and tried to use that sermon and text to let people know that just because the Bible talks about slavery, no, they don't need to throw their entire faith away!

We also talk about things like homosexuality, divorce, sex before marriage, all things that *I'm sure* make people leave our church. I've read their emails. But I have to remember that Jesus didn't tell me to attract a crowd! Jesus told me to scatter seed. And Jesus told me that some people's hearts are soil where seed cannot grow. So my job is to do my job, let Jesus do his, and pray that people accept it while understanding that many of them will not.

To wrap up this chapter, let me just remind you again. We need God's word to succeed. And of course, the Bible is not our Savior. Jesus is our Savior, Jesus is the one who died for us and rose again. So I don't want to lift the Bible up to an idolatrous level that it's not intended to be. The Bible didn't save me, Jesus did. However, the data, and my experience, and Jesus' own words all show that if we stay faithful to the Bible we will see in people the transformation that we so long for, that Jesus calls us to make, and for which we started our churches.

Chapter 12

MY SECRET

I remember the day I realized I was right.

Out of college, I had worked at a church plant for 4 years. It was fun and grueling, as we struggled to grow as a church. When the megachurch hired me as their "resident church planter" one of the many things I was excited about was the chance to learn the right way to do things. This huge church was successful by all counts—humongous and still growing, large offerings, nice buildings, humble leadership. So when I went on staff, I may not have phrased it this way, but I thought, "Now I can figure out the right way to do things."

Within my first couple months on staff at the huge church, I had just that chance. They were launching a huge new groups initiative. In an effort to connect more people with each other, they were starting a new system of getting into and leading groups. When I first heard it I was very skeptical of the idea. I knew it had worked at other churches, but it didn't seem like a great cultural fit. But the new small groups' minister had written books on small groups, spoke at conferences, and was respected around the country as a groups guru. So I trusted him.

Fast forward six months, when I heard the number of people who had gotten into groups and realized: I was right! That system had not worked well. In fact, for the amount of money and time that was spent on it, you could probably classify it as a total failure.

It was then that I had an epiphany: these people don't know what they're doing either! Now I had never had a staff person arrogantly say they did know what they're doing. But I had just assumed since the church was successful in any way we could measure success in the American church that they knew better than others how to do things. I had been looking for a magic pill that I could take to my church plant and instantly make us grow. The problem was that pill doesn't exist.

In fact, one time I was talking with the co-preacher at this church and I asked why he didn't go to conferences at other churches. His response? "They don't know what they're doing either!" He pointed out that there were different seasons that it was important for him to go to such conferences, but the reason he went was more for spiritual growth and not to learn how to do ministry.

So here's my secret: **I don't know what I'm doing.** I've saved this bit of information until this chapter so I'd get you to read a little bit first. I'm guessing if I started the book with this not many of you would have made it to this point.

So if you have read something you disagree with or think is heresy or you just know is wrong, you may be right. It's up to you to wisely figure out what contrarian wisdom fits your context and what doesn't.

> # The good news: Nobody else knows what they're doing either.

Everyone is making it up as they go along. The problem with a lot of books and conferences is that they relate what worked in their context, and we assume it will work in ours. Please know that I don't think those authors or speakers have bad intentions. I don't necessarily think that they're trying to sell something they don't believe in. In fact, most church conferences I've been to they'll give a speech at the beginning explaining that they don't have everything figured out and that the last thing they want you to do is to make a carbon copy of their church. However, after three days of being immersed in their culture, that's often what the attendees want to do.

The conventional practice is to figure out the "right" way to do church. We'll read books, attend conferences, and listen to podcasts, all in the name of figuring out the right way to do things. But the bottom line is that no one knows what they're doing.

***

Pretty often I'll have a conversation that I love. An

aspiring church planter will contact me to ask what they should do in the pre-launch phase to meet people. They have heard that we launched successfully and obviously, they want to do the same thing, so they are looking for advice on how to imitate us. I laugh and say, "I hope God blesses it." The response is always: "Yeah, I know that, but what practical things would you say?" I laugh again and say, "You don't get it. We tried a ton of things, and just about all of them failed!"

My wife joined a moms' group to meet other moms. They all lived far away and had no interest. Fail.

I joined the chamber of commerce in an effort to meet other business leaders. When they found out I was a pastor and couldn't offer them any business, they avoided me like the plague. Well, the guy who was trying to get pot legalized wanted to hang out. Fail.

The first six months on the ground we didn't have any kind of office, so local coffee shops and cafes were my "office". The plan was that I'd meet the workers and customers there and invite them to join us. You know how many of the hundreds I met at those places attended a single launch team meeting? Zero. Fail.

Do you want me to keep going?

We spent $5,000 on advertisements that showed before the movies in the theatre where we were going to meet. You know how many people came because of those ads? Four. Heck, I could've walked around the mall and paid people a thousand bucks each to visit Mosaic and gotten better results. Fail.

We tried to have a neighborhood cookout. We put

flyers on the doors of the hundred houses on our street, advertising a free cookout put on by the newest neighbors on the street. We had hot dogs, sodas and a moon bounce, set up in our front yard. You know how many people came? Two. And they left pretty quickly when they realized they were the only ones. Fail.

I could keep going, but I'll quit while I'm ahead.

In spite of failure, I wouldn't go back and change any of those things. To explain why I'll quote Mark Batterson: Everything is an experiment. That's one of the core values of National Community Church, and now Mosaic has adopted it into our culture. Everything is an experiment. Think of the freedom that gives you to try new things, to fail, to stretch yourself, to question. Here's what Mark points out:

> "At the end of your ministry, you won't regret the mistakes you made nearly as much as the opportunities you missed. That conviction is based on the research of two sociologists, Tom Gilovich and Vicki Medvec. According to their study, time is a key factor in what we regret. In the short-term, we tend to regret our actions. Action regrets outnumber inaction regrets 53 percent to 47 percent during an average week. Over the long-haul, however, we tend to regret inactions. When people look at their lives as a whole, inaction regrets outnumber action regrets 84 percent to 16 percent."

A problem in church planting is that there is an entire church planting machine out there that can give you the impression that you know what you're doing. I recently asked church plant guru Ed Stetzer what has changed now from when he launched the first of the six churches he planted. One of the main differences, he said, is that you can have the "machine" do much of the work for you. So you can advertise, get equipment, rent space, become a legal non-profit, and many other things just by using different companies' services. Those are a good thing, but Ed pointed out we still have to love our neighbor. He then went through every house on his street and explained where they are spiritually. Some are having conversations, one is a leader in his church, and one hates him!

The "machine" of church planting is very helpful; I have used most of it. But it can give you the impression that you know what you're doing and if you just go through this checklist of things you'll have a great church.

There are three implications of this idea that no one knows what they are doing. They are principles that we must live out.

Principle #1: Default to Action

There are times to read books and go to conferences, but there comes a time to plant. It's that time when you realize that no church is going to be perfect, so you're going to do the best you can. Yes, it may fail. No, it will not be perfect. Yes, you will look back and be embarrassed about some things you did. But no, you will not stand before God one day and say you did nothing. Remember the parable of the talents. Both the five-talent guy and the two-talent guy put the master's money to work, and they ended up doubling it. The one-talent guy acted in fear. It was like he wanted to find the perfect investment before he did anything with his master's money. The end result is that he faced condemnation.

One time I heard a skeptic raking a church leader through the coals about his philosophy of ministry. The pastor patiently listened. After explaining that the critic did indeed have some good points he said, "But I like the way we're doing it better than the way you're not doing it."

It's easy to criticize, but the best criticism is through creativity, which necessitates action. Oscar Wilde said that the difference between an amateur author and a professional author is that the amateur has the luxury of writing only when the muses strike, but the professional author must get up and write, whether he feels like it or not. I think that's the attitude we need to have in church planting. And I think it's what we see in great followers of God in the Bible:

Jonathan didn't wait for a call from God but attacked the Philistines, igniting a rout of the pagans brought by God. Esther recognized that she had been born for the very moment of speaking up to the king on behalf of her people. Abraham didn't know where he was going, but he followed God anyway.

Someone has said that "faith" is spelled R-I-S-K. Know that you may lose it all, but if you aren't willing to risk your reputation, your intellect, your finances, your professional future, do you really have faith?

What risk do you need to take? What step of faith do you need to take? Do you have faith?

Principle #2 Stay humble

Every part of the church plant journey invites you to be proud because every success is so monumental. You moved to a new city...be proud of that. You recruited your first launch team member...be proud. You baptized your first convert...be proud. You crossed the 100/200/500 barrier...be proud. Those are all great things!

It's tough to be proud of what God is doing and stay humble about yourself at the same time, though, so recognize now that you probably think more highly of yourself than you ought to. In fact, I think this is why so many church resources aren't as helpful as we'd wish because they have what has been dubbed "the halo effect". Essentially the halo effect says that once an event has been a success we look back on it more affectionately. Therefore, we remember all the reasons it went right and we forget all the things that went wrong, and we forget that we may have done the same things in other instances yet didn't replicate the success.

My favorite business book is *Good to Great*. I think it contains invaluable wisdom for many endeavors, including church planting. But now that it has been around a few years, look at what's happened to several of the companies Jim Collins profiled in that book:

Circuit City: bankrupt. Fannie Mae: bankrupt and nationalized. Wells Fargo: Needs another $13 billion. Nucor: Stock and Revenue crashed down 50 percent. Pitney Bowes: Stock and Revenue crashed down 15 percent. Gillette: No longer independent.

The companies we were learning from in 2001 are struggling big time now. What happened? Well, it could be that the book is a farce, and the halo effect was probably in effect for this book, as it is for all business books. But I think the book itself hits on a key principle of growth. One of the CEOs, when asked why his company had done so well, simply said, "We got lucky."

Wow. That is humility and honesty. And I know what you're thinking—surely they did something that made them successful. I mean, that's why we buy the book so we can learn that stuff. And they've done some good things for sure, but at the end of the day, they got lucky. The way the Christian would say this is "God blessed it."

Think of the parable of the sower. God controls the sun and the rain. All we can do is scatter seed—that is literally the one thing we have control over. We scatter it wherever we can, even in obscure places, hoping and praying it will take root. Then we hope and pray that God will provide enough sun and rain to make it grow. But at the end of the day, we really have no control over whether it grows or not.

If we remember that, it will keep us humble because we'll realize all we really have is the hope that God will provide.

Principle #3 Defined by Love

We talked about this last chapter, but let me say one more thing about this. This is the key. This is it. If you miss this, you miss everything.

A few years ago, our church started a "Love Week" similar to what we've seen other churches do. Essentially, we blitz our community with dozens of service projects over the course of seven days. Our church goes nuts with it—service projects fill up, people take off work, kids serve—it's amazing.

Recently I preached on a weekend at the end of Love Week and said that I get a lot of questions about our church's and my personal responses to things wrong in our state, specifically racism and community/church relations. Well, this week was our response. Our response isn't a speech or a Scripture; our response is an action. Jesus said we would know who follows him by their love. So that's who we will be. If we do that, we're on the right track. If we don't love others, it doesn't matter what we say.

Now Start!

I remember the call like it was yesterday. I was working out at home before my wife returned home from work. Then my phone rang. I recognized the area code and assumed someone in my family had gotten a new cell phone, so I answered the call that set my life on a new trajectory.

A couple of months earlier I had run into an old friend at the Exponential church planting conference. There I had pitched to him the idea that his church should hire someone as a resident church planter to learn from them for a year before heading out to plant. So on a sunny afternoon after finishing my workout I answered a call from that church and had a cool conversation that left me stunned, speechless, and scared.

My wife got home, and as we piled into the car to head to dinner, I still didn't have words to communicate. Finally, after we had sat down in our favorite Mexican restaurant and were eating the chips and salsa, I broke the news:

"We've been asked to plant a church." I explained the situation: they wanted to hire me as the resident church planter. So we had the opportunity to move to another city for a year and following that, to relocate to a city where we would plant a church from scratch. My voice quivered and my hands trembled as I shared the news. I knew the journey we were getting ready to embark on would be the most difficult task of our lives. It would stretch our faith, it would exhaust us physically, it would test the limits of our marriage, it would test our resolve, it would refine us like fire. It has done all those things, and more.   And it's been the greatest ride I've ever been a part of.

I want you to experience the same ride. God has called you to church planting. You need to be wise, and have faith hope and love as your guiding principles. It will push you to new heights and lows in your faith, and you will get to be a part of the great mission of bringing God's lost children home. God is with you. He will never leave you. He will never forsake you.   So go do this thing. Today your journey is starting.

You are already a contrarian. Now become a contrarian church planter.

Coaching & Speaking

Church planting is in the heart of Carl Kuhl, and he desires to see new churches planted and grow. To this end, he offers coaching of a select number of planters each year, as well as a limited number of dates to speak to church planters. To inquire about coaching or speaking, email carl@mosaicchristian.org.

Printed by Amazon Italia Logistica S.r.l.
Torrazza Piemonte (TO), Italy

11416522R00121